Fortune & Freedom: The Entrepreneur's Guide to Success breaks down all of the essential steps of becoming a successful entrepreneur, using great anecdotes and insight. The book definitely helped me look in the mirror and see ways I can be more efficient and successful.

—CRAIG BAERWALDT, PRESIDENT
ALLSTATE INSURANCE
CASCADIA AGENCY

My first business, while successful, would have been so much easier had I had the incredible insights provided in *Fortune & Freedom*. Jim Hirshfield outlines a perfect model for success in both business and family life.

—ERIC DOBSON, FORMER CEO, ETD INVESTMENTS

The book helped take the "largeness" out of my new business and showed me how to simply focus on the basic, most important aspects of getting it up and running.

—JODIE REINERTSON, MD

James Hirshfield shares his strategic insights as well as his practical tips on being an entrepreneur and creating the good life.

—BOYD WATKINS, PRESIDENT
REALTY WEST PROPERTIES

I'm not an entrepreneur. I joined an entrepreneur, Bill Moog, when his company had a thousand employees and sales of $25 million. Twenty-two years later, at $300 million, Bill retired and I became CEO. Moog Inc. is now close to $2 billion.

Jim Hirshfield's advice wasn't available for us at the time — but it resonates now. Jim is adamant that you've got to have a plan. Jim talks about the C-word, commitment. Our plans would not have succeeded without our relentless commitment. And, as Jim suggests, when you get your company started, you're responsible for the culture. Bill took ownership for developing a company culture that my management team has embraced and elaborated. All the way along, we have made time for our personal lives and commitments. The career plan that Jim presents worked for Bill Moog and for me.

I hope it works for you.

—ROBERT T. BRADY, CEO, MOOG INC.

I'm pretty blown away by the breadth of the material you cover in such a short book.

—RICHARD CHEN, MAJOR, USA (RET)

Your book really impacted my decision making.

—NIKESH PAREKH, VICE PRESIDENT
HOUSEVALUES, INC.

SOLID ADVICE YOU CAN USE
FROM A GUY WHO'S BEEN THERE

If you are considering pursuing an entrepreneurial enterprise or already stand at the helm of one, here is information that will help you reach your goals with ease and confidence. *Fortune & Freedom: The Entrepreneur's Guide to Success*, starts with ideas for people just beginning their business life and ends with tips on how to prepare for life after the company is sold. In between is a veritable gold mine of practical wisdom — keys to prospering in the entrepreneurial world.

Fortune & Freedom: The Entrepreneur's Guide to Success presents complex points with crystal clarity and simplicity. Each chapter ends with a review and suggestions for next steps. At every stage you know what to look for and what to do when you find it.

You will learn:

- It is not how much you earn but how much you spend that determines your financial situation.
- Investors need to invest somewhere. They need you as much as you need them. They want to put their money with someone who will respect their investment.
- Controlling the deal is controlling your future.
- It's not just about profit. What's important is building value.
- When you are young, time seems a plentiful asset. On the other side of the middle of life, time is *the* non-replaceable asset.

Gems like these are what this book delivers. Use it as a hands-on resource, and keep it within easy reach.

A successful entrepreneur for more than thirty years, Jim Hirshfield stands on a bedrock of experience. In 1973 he founded Summit Communications, Inc., a cable company that grew to employ 130 people. He was the CEO for twenty-six years until he sold the prospering company he had built. Jim chose the entrepreneur's path so he could engage in a challenging business career, spend quality time with his family, and do philanthropic work as well. He has been eminently effective at all three. Jim and his wife, Mary, have been married for almost forty years and have three adult children. Jim writes, consults, speaks, sails, and generally has a great life. He divides his time between his homes in Washington State and Hawaii.

FORTUNE & FREEDOM

The Entrepreneur's Guide to Success

FORTUNE & FREEDOM

The Entrepreneur's Guide to Success

JIM HIRSHFIELD

MILLENNIUM
VENTURES PRESS

MILLENNIUM
VENTURES PRESS

2760 76th Ave SE Suite 508
Mercer Island, WA 98040
Tel: 425.747-2198 • Fax: 425. 957-1293
www.millenniumventurespress.com

This publication is designed to provide accurate and authoritative information in regard to the subject matter covered. It is not intended to
replace the counsel of professional advisers. While the author has taken
reasonable precautions in the preparation of this book and believes the
facts presented within the book are accurate, neither the publisher nor
author assumes any responsibility for errors or omissions. The author and
publisher specifically disclaim any liability resulting from the use or
application of the information contained in this book.

Publisher's Cataloguing-in-Publication information:

Hirshfield, James A.

    Fortune & freedom : the entrepreneur's guide to success / Jim
Hirshfield. -- 1st ed. -- Mercer Island, WA : Millennium Ventures Press,
2008.
        p. ; cm.
        ISBN: 978-0-9798127-0-5 (pbk. : alk. paper)
    1. Entrepreneurship. 2. New business enterprises. 3. Success
in business. I. Title. II. Title: Fortune and freedom.
III. Entrepreneur's guide to success.

    HB615 .H57 2008   2007935662
    338.04/092--dc22   0801

Author Photo: Alex Rubin
Cover & Book Design: Patricia Bacall
Book & Publishing Consultant: Ellen Reid

Printed in the United States of America on acid-free paper

For Mary

CONTENTS

FOREWORD

At Harvard Business School our mission is to educate leaders who make a difference in the world. We draw bright young men and women together and ask them to study a wide range of problems. Within this rich soup of talent, brains, and experience our students become more educated in the application of leadership through a broad range of situations. While going through this intense program we remind students not to lose sight of the forest for the trees — this book reinforces that.

Jim Hirshfield went through the program at HBS. He maintained his focus and further honed it during the decades of his very successful entrepreneurial career. Now he has written a simple book that focuses on the key issues of entrepreneurship. This book is written for the entrepreneur as a person, rather than the entrepreneurial business being created. Success is something which is achieved both in business and with family, Jim says. It is not measured by a specific business venture but over a lifetime.

Jim first sets out the importance of planning, noting that "if you don't know where you are going, any road is the right road." He then discusses skills which an entrepreneur will require. But where should you spend your time? Which skills are most important? Jim suggests a short list for consideration.

The main factors in doing a deal to get into business are discussed, starting with the quote "If your ship doesn't come in, should you swim out to it?" And then, when you are in business, what are the issues in successfully operating your venture?

Jim gives you keys to successful execution of your business plan. Finally, Jim notes that an exit plan will exist for your business, and it will be a better plan if you craft it yourself versus just letting it happen.

With the goal of addressing just key issues, Jim has purposefully kept this book short. You will find it difficult to get lost in the detail here. The main points stand out and are well illustrated by stories from Jim's career. This book is practical, powerful, and to the point.

WILLIAM A. SAHLMAN
SENIOR ASSOCIATE DEAN, EXTERNAL RELATIONS
PROFESSOR, ENTREPRENEURIAL FINANCE
HARVARD GRADUATE SCHOOL OF BUSINESS ADMINISTRATION

PREFACE

*W*ebster's Dictionary says an entrepreneur is "a person who organizes and manages an enterprise, esp. a business, usu. with considerable initiative and risk." I used to tell people that an entrepreneur is someone who pays wages to others on a regular basis and always makes the payroll. If you can make a payroll, you get to make a lot of the decisions affecting how you run your business and your life. You get to be free. I was an entrepreneur for over thirty years, and enjoyed the freedom it brought me in my business and in my personal life.

Why am I qualified to write this guide? Here is my story:

My father was a career military officer, and growing up I had little knowledge or understanding of business. After completing college and serving in the Navy, I decided to go into business. I worked for a year, went back to Harvard Business School, then launched my career in business. In 1966, when I entered the cable television industry at age twenty-seven, I had never earned over $3,000 in a year. In 1999, when I retired and sold Summit Communications, the company I had founded twenty-six years earlier, we had over 40,000 customers and were a significant player in the cable television industry. As more fully detailed in my biography at the back of this book, I had been a "success." During those thirty-three years, I had employed as many as 130 people, operated businesses in seven Western states, and had built, purchased, and sold over fifty businesses in several communications-related industries. At age sixty-one I asked for my Social Security statement. It came with earnings noted for each of the previous forty-five years. That is a lot of years spent developing approaches to the problems encountered in business and in life. In this book I share those approaches with you.

This book is also about how I achieved freedom. In relating what worked for me in mapping my road to success, I wanted to give you new approaches to consider when you find you are up against new problems. It is not intended to be an all-inclusive primer. Rather, think of this book as a weekend "clinic." It concentrates on the key issues that seemed to be the primary determinants of my success, and gives you my approach to those issues.

One of my life goals was to be successful both financially and in my family life. I am particularly pleased that our three children each completed college in four years, picked up a couple of master's degrees, and are all gainfully employed in fields that excite and motivate them. I know a lot of people who have been successful financially, and I know a lot of people who have fine families. I know fewer people who have done both. I used to schedule school conferences, Boy Scout meetings, and similar events on the same calendar where I scheduled my business meetings. Coming home after a day at work, I felt there was nothing finer than getting down on the floor to play with my kids. You can be highly successful in both your business and in your family life. But it does not come automatically. It is a choice.

My father, a career U.S. Coast Guard officer, used to say, "Different ships, different long splices." He was referring to splicing lines—joining together two ropes at their ends—and saying that there are many different ways to complete a task effectively or to produce a desired result. For that matter, there is always a diverse range of desired results. There is no single "right" way.

In this book I talk about the ways that worked for me. I lay out the rules, guidelines, and principles that helped me to successfully execute my life. They worked for me as an entrepreneur, and I believe they will be useful to you as well.

INTRODUCTION

My objective is to help you achieve the freedom you seek as an entrepreneur while living a balanced life. You will find this guide useful whether you have not yet embarked on your entrepreneurial career or are right in the middle of it. Problems arise every day. This book is a place you can go in search of answers.

To be an entrepreneur you need to function at a consistent, steady level amid the stress of business deals, day-to-day operations, and your personal life. As you do this, you will enhance your freedom to act on your own timetable, both in business and in life.

In 1968, at age thirty, I had an opportunity to buy a small cable TV company. I felt ready. I quit my job as chief financial officer of a medium-sized company and went to work full time in my own cable TV business. My wife, Mary, and I signed a contract to buy this cable TV business, using a note of $30,000 for the down payment. My annual salary was less than half that amount. Immediately after the signing, Mary drove me to the airport. I was headed to Boston to raise the money to complete the purchase.

"If you do not raise the money," she said slowly, "how will we pay off the note? We don't have $30,000."

"Don't worry," I replied, and got out of the car to catch my plane.

Of course, we had reason to worry, but she supported me, we executed well in a stressful situation, we got the financial commitment, and I closed the deal. I left my job and started in as a full-time small businessman. I owned 20 percent of the company (later reduced to 17 percent through dilution). My venture capital partners in Boston owned the balance. I raised a million dollars of institutional debt in New York and started to build my cable TV business.

Four years later the company had grown significantly and my venture capital partners wanted to liquidate. As a good steward of their financial interests, I sold the company. I shook hands with the senior vice president of Teleprompter Corporation on a stock swap at $41 a share. We closed the sale two months later in New York, right after Christmas. Teleprompter stock was $36 a share. The next summer, the stock was selling at $1.50 per share. The chairman was going to jail, top management had turned over, and everything was in turmoil. My nest egg was gone. I had just turned thirty-four, had two children and a mortgage, and was starting again. I decided I would never do another stock deal.

This lesson and others shaped my experience as an entrepreneur. In *Fortune & Freedom,* I lay out approaches to important issues you will encounter as an entrepreneur. My approach to these issues is a result of my own experience.

PART I: SUCCESS

*If you do not know where you are going,
you will get there.*

We all want to be "successful." In our early years we often do not know what that means. It is easy to go to work in an organization and accept that organization's definition of success: Do this project for two years, do it well, and you will move up to the next grade, and so forth. We look to our parents, mentors, and other older people we believe "did well" and use them to define success (which is a moving target if the older person does not have a thoughtful definition on which he or she relies). Or we just wander through life without letting this definitional problem worry us.

CHAPTER 1

WHERE IS THE END OF THE RAINBOW?

Twenty-nine years ago, having recently bought our present home, I was out in the front yard one hot summer evening wrapping up my day's work. I was installing a sprinkler system prior to putting in the lawn. I had spent the day running the rented trenching machine, cutting plastic pipe, and laying out fittings at the necessary places. I was gluing the last of the lot as daylight faded. Needless to say, I was pretty grimy, the dust and dirt mixing with my perspiration throughout the day.

A late-model, expensive car pulled up to the curb, and a fellow perhaps ten years younger than I jumped out. He was of medium height, with a boyish face and blond hair, and he was wearing a shirt and tie, but no jacket. Sort of the John Kennedy campaign look. Holding a clipboard in his hand, he came over to where I was working.

"Could I ask you some questions?" he said. He explained that he was taking a course on how to be a success. I said I would be pleased to answer his survey questions, as long as I could keep working while doing so. I asked why he had chosen me to interview.

"This neighborhood has nice homes," he said, "and I chose it because the people living in these homes must be successful." I pointed out that his car was about ten years newer than the one in the driveway belonging to me, that he was certainly dressed better than I, and that someone driving by would likely assume he was the homeowner and I was the hired help.

I do not know if he got the message I was trying to deliver. We did his survey. I do not remember anything in particular about the survey, but I clearly remember the incident. What constitutes success? How did this guy define success? He was taking a course. I was covered in dirt, working. His approach to success was certainly different than mine! But I was the guy who was free.

Defining Success for Yourself

In our early married years Mary and I used to go to the occasional neighborhood party, attended by people pretty much like us, living in similar circumstances. They dressed well (better than I) and presented themselves as being very successful in their careers. A few years later many of these families were in disarray as a result of things such as career problems, money problems, midlife crises, drinking and other addictions, and divorce. Simply said, the people so affected were largely drifting along without considering where they wanted to end up. For many, the trip through life became a journey from hell.

Some years ago I was at a meeting when a fellow a few years younger than I, with whom I used to work, approached. His family had a number of businesses, and he had done quite well with them since he had taken over as CEO a number of years earlier. He came over to thank me for saying something to him years earlier when we had worked together.

"You told me," he said, "that if you don't know where you are going, any road is the right road. That comment stuck with me and has made a big difference in my life." Needless to say, I was flattered. People generally do not thank you for offering advice. I did not remember the earlier discussion but thought I probably had made the comment to try to help him over a rough patch at the company.

> *. . . if you don't know where you are going, any road is the right road.*

The principle I expressed in that bit of advice is very important. If you have your long-term goals in mind and you are progressing toward them, then the other day-to-day stuff is an irritant with which you can deal.

Defining success is crucial in almost anything you do, including business deals, working with people, and the many day-to-day decisions involved in business. How can you be free if you do not define what that means?

Setting Goals

My goal was to be a financial success without sacrificing family or community service. My financial goal was to create value over the long term. My personal goal was to develop a fine family over the long term. While doing these things, I also wanted to provide service to my community.

As I thought about how to achieve my goals, I believed that when faced with a choice, a good tactic was to try to opt for the alternative that created options rather than foreclosed them. That is, I tried to do work and other activities that opened up further options for work and activities, as opposed to taking the choice that did not lead to anything further.

Like all things, goals are relative. No family is perfect, and someone will always be richer than you. So be realistic, and forgive yourself if you notice a few people who seem to be doing better. You will find that in the short run things are not always what they seem, and in the long run we all end up the same.

Mapping Out Your Plan

How do you go about laying out a plan for success? Again, "different ships, different long splices." Just as there are many ways to define success, there are also many ways to seek it. What worked for me was a process I undertook for several years in my mid-twenties. Twice a year I sat down to put in writing my definition of success, my assets and liabilities in pursuing it, and the skills I would require in order to get there.

At first this was a real helter-skelter process. Over time, however, I found that certain things remained in my document, while other things came and went. These core items that persisted became my definition, my goal.

My structure for this process involved listing categories such as the following and using them as an outline for my document:

Personal Assets:

- What are my personal strengths and weaknesses?
- What do I do well, what do I do poorly? Which of the latter must I improve?

Personal Desires:

- What would I most enjoy spending my waking hours doing?
- How much money do I want to make in the future?
- Do I want to manage people or not?

Family Desires:

- How do I want my family life to develop?
- Where do I want to live?

Future Images:

- What is the mental picture of a day in my life ten years hence? Twenty years?

KEY POINTS

- *Define what you will consider as success, your definition of the freedom you seek.*
- *Do not allow others to define success for you.*
- *Define your goals.*
- *Prepare a detailed "how-to" list for mapping out your plan for success.*

WHAT TO DO

Sit down and write out your plan for success. Six months later, do it again. Compare the two. Six months later, write another. Keep it up until the changes you make are small.

CHAPTER 2

TRAINING FOR THE SUMMIT

Having defined success, do you think it will roll down the street and pull into your driveway? Probably not. If you hope to achieve freedom and success as you have defined them, what skills, talents, and abilities will you need along the way to do your part to make it happen? And, just as important, what are the precepts, the moral and ethical framework, within which you wish to live your life?

Skills

Over the years I have always spent time talking with younger people about their career paths. They often do not like the input they receive from me, because I suggest they work at a nitty-gritty level over the next few years to obtain a set of skills. I suggest that they sell vacuum cleaners door to door, manage a shift at a fast-food restaurant, manage the finances for a volunteer organization, and be active in a political campaign. What I try to do is suggest ways they can acquire skills they will need to move along the road to success, and define the precepts they will follow to guide their lives.

Obtaining the necessary skills is important but perhaps difficult, because to get them you may have to postpone nice things that you would otherwise be able to get sooner, things that you might find quite gratifying. The desire for instant gratification can be a real barrier to freedom.

> *The desire for instant gratification can be a real barrier to freedom.*

The son of a friend of mine thought he was going to be a success. He dropped out of college because he was not moving along fast enough toward his goal of being an entrepreneur. Unfortunately, his parents were well off, and they supported his ventures. And supported them. And supported them. He had no long-term plan for success, nor did he have the basket of skills necessary for success. Ten years later he is still looking for his next business venture, having failed in several to date.

Precepts

In addition to developing skills, it is important to consider your *precepts*—the moral and ethical stances that shape how you approach your work and your life. In my definition of precepts I also include non-work-related issues that are important to you, things that bear on whatever you want to do with your life in order to achieve your definition of success. For example, if family is important to you, then you should focus on what matters in that arena as well. Chapter 3 provides a detailed discussion of precepts.

Getting Up to Bat

It is axiomatic in baseball that you cannot get a hit unless you get up to bat. The same is true of your career, your plan for success, or your entrepreneurial venture. As you move through life, give yourself a chance to get some hits. Take the steps in building your career that will allow you to get up to bat. Take a job that allows you to manage people. Learn how to sell. Learn about the role of money in our economy. Expose yourself to politics. Practice leadership.

It is axiomatic in baseball that you cannot get a hit unless you get up to bat.

Location, Industry, and Functional Skills

Location, industry, and functional skills make up a useful triangle to consider. Discussing this triangle briefly at this point will help set the stage for Part II of this book, where I discuss functional skills at some length.

If where you live—your *location*—is important to you, some opportunities will be more available than others, and they perhaps will require a specific mix of skills. For instance, working in the steel industry will qualify you for a very narrow range of opportunities if you want to live in Seattle.

Industry-based knowledge, gained by working in a specific industry over time, is useful in that industry, but sometimes is less useful when you try to move to other industries. That is, if you are in Seattle and are dedicated to becoming a steel company executive, you will find yourself moving to other states. As your career progresses, you will find fewer and fewer opportunities outside of the steel industry.

A basic *functional skill* such as accounting, sales, production, or information systems translates much more easily among industries and among locations.

I believe that a career can contain any two, but hardly ever all three, of these items. Location and industry are often at odds because industry-specific opportunities will invariably present themselves at some other location. Functional skills are more easily transferable. If your goal is to be an entrepreneur, you must develop functional skills as part of your triangle.

If you want to live in a particular location that is more or less a "company town," then functional skills may be less important than the other two legs of my triangle. I am not sure living in a company town with your livelihood reliant on a single provider is a good long-run decision, however, and it will work against your entrepreneurial aspirations. If a town is dominated by a single large company, most of the entrepreneurial opportunities there will involve doing business with that corporation and the industry it represents.

So once again we come to functional skills. If you want to live in a location with a range of business opportunities, then a functional specialty is important. If you are uncertain, developing a functional specialty will probably best maximize your future opportunities.

Basic functional skills, such as selling, finance, people management, and more, apply over a broad range of opportunities. Other areas that may appear to be functional fields are actually career dead ends, in my opinion. Usually they are the so-called "soft" version of one of the functional fields. For instance, *inside sales*, which involves doing administrative work for the direct sales force that is out calling on customers, may be a useful step toward an outside direct-selling opportunity. Or it might simply be sales administration, which requires you to do low-level administrative tasks into the foreseeable future, working in the sales functional field without ever learning how to sell. *Event planning* is another favorite example of mine. Someone else makes the sale and you put the event together, functioning as a skilled administrator who can talk with people. It is a fun job in your twenties, but where does it lead you in terms of functional skills you can apply to a career as an entrepreneur or a high-level company employee?

The Wide Applicability of Functional Skills

CPAs can almost always get a job, because they represent the gold standard for accounting, and every organization needs someone to account for the money. A good direct salesperson can sell almost anything; a mediocre direct sales person can still make a living. People management is a critical skill. How scary would it be to get your big break at age forty or fifty, have several hundred or thousand people working for you, and never have had any experience managing people? Functional skills are important not only to your entrepreneurial quest, but also to any kind of career in business or in any type of organization.

Commitment—The Old "C" Word

In my mid-twenties I was fortunate to be able to attend the Harvard Graduate School of Business Administration. The program really tested one's ability to deal with uncertainty. We started in September and got our first grades in March. None of us really knew how we were doing until that time. Yes, we had an idea, but the school worked to keep the pressure on. We had been told that about 10 percent of our classmates would not make it through the first year. My roommate Harry Mosle and I adopted a practical approach. We counted nine people in our section of ninety who were likely to go before us, and then we stopped worrying about it.

Interestingly, we felt they were likely to leave not because they lacked brain power, but because of their lack of commitment—the old "C" word. Throughout my life I have often found the "C" word to be the difference between success and failure.

Do not confuse commitment with academic excellence. Yes, you should work hard to learn necessary skills. But do not be discouraged if others get the high grades. When I was in the navy, the commanding officer of my ship was Ernie Cornwall, who had been last in his class at the U.S. Naval Academy. One day he said, "Jim, do you remember the captain we met last night at the officers' club?"

I said, "Yes, sir," and noted that Ernie was a commander, junior to a captain.

"Do you see that old ship over there?"

I looked at the twenty-year-old destroyer, much older and smaller than ours, very beat up, and close to retirement.

"Yes, sir."

"He is skipper of that ship," Ernie said. "He was first in my class at Annapolis." Then Ernie lowered his hat over his eyes and sat back in his chair, smiling. Ernie was last in his class, but he had gotten the job done. He had committed to his success. He commanded the brand-new destroyer.

KEY POINTS

- *Prepare for success.*
- *Develop your skill sets and thinking about precepts.*
- *Be sure to "get up to bat."*
- *Be aware of the trade-offs among location, industry, and functional skills.*
- *Recognize the importance of functional skills.*
- *Don't forget commitment—the old "C" word.*

WHAT TO DO

Commit to a program of acquiring the skills you must acquire to deliver your future success. Part II of this book discusses the important ones at greater length.

CHAPTER 3

WHO ARE YOU, ANYWAY?

Michael Porter, a Harvard Business School professor, says a strategy is defined by the things you choose *not* to do. He is talking about business, but the same is true of personal strategies. What price are you willing to pay for the freedom you will have as a successful entrepreneur? What kind of person do you wish to be? What lessons do you wish to pass on to your children (who always do what you do, not what you say)? When your life ends, how do you wish to be remembered? This section discusses the need to surface the things you choose to do and not do as you go about defining your strategy for success. Many of these things deal with ethics and morals.

> *. . . a strategy is defined by the things you choose not to do.*

Why make them explicit? Some people have a better moral compass than others. Even people with a strong moral compass can get sidetracked, I believe, when stress and the press of events hurry them past important decision points.

Our society tends to forgive these failings, as the following anecdote illustrates. I had an employee steal from our company. We terminated him and offset his last paycheck by the amount that he had stolen from us. He took us to court to recover those offset wages. The judge agreed he had stolen from us but sided with him, citing his lack of resources and his difficult personal situation, which "drove" him to liberate a few of our assets. No one will ever cause this fellow to deal with his own moral issues. He will have to do so himself.

How do you wish to be viewed? What things fall outside the boundaries of acceptable behavior, and how will you know when you are crossing those lines as you go through life? It is not uncommon in business and organizations to have an issue that is both economic and ethical. Unbundling these and dealing with them can be difficult.

If you reach your entrepreneurial goal of leading an organization, you will find that the people who work there reflect your precepts. They will be like your children in that they will do what you do, not what you say. What kind of people do you want to attract to your organization? What is the face you want your organization to present to your community?

A friend and I were talking about a third guy, a fellow who had just seen his business collapse. His investors had pretty much lost everything, but he had been able to hold on to his multimillion-dollar home. I asked my friend how long he thought it would be before this fellow could get back on his feet in the business world.

"How long does it take to regain your good name?" he replied. His implication, of course, was that you can never erase certain actions and recover your good name.

Not all precepts raise ethical issues. Some may simply be trade-offs. Do your spouse and children always come first? Do you simply refuse to move to another city? Do you decline to ever do manual labor? The list goes on. As you consider precepts, carefully analyze the trade-offs they present to your plan for success. You will always face trade-offs. The trick is to reconcile them to your plan.

Here are some other specific issues that should find their way into your plan for success.

The role of family is likely to be a key part of your plan. If you want to have a spouse and children, do you care where they live or how often they have to move? (My older sister attended twelve different schools before graduating from high school.) Do you care about how much time they get to spend with you and your spouse? How high a rating do you give the importance of your family versus your career?

Will your spouse also have a career? What trade-offs will the two of you have to face in this event? Many people make decisions by default and later in life do not like the consequences of those decisions. Realize that a decision is being made. Do it affirmatively with your spouse, and you will not wake up one morning some years in the future wondering why life has brought you to your present situation.

Your time. Realize there are only so many hours in the day. Your most important asset is your time. In fact, the goal of achieving freedom as an entrepreneur is really a goal to return more hours to you, which you can then apply as you deem

> *Your most important asset is your time.*

most useful. I used to schedule family time and events just like a business meeting on my calendar. When I worked for other people, I used a code in case someone checked my calendar. I considered a family commitment the most important type of meeting I could have and did not allow others to schedule something else for me in that time. Occasionally this caused problems, but I knew where my priorities were.

Your health. Your body is the only place you have in which to live. It seems obvious that you will not be able to execute your plan if you die early. You probably will not be able to execute your plan if your health is impaired and you have less energy to apply to your career. Although we never know when something might happen to us, we can definitely lower the probability of bad medical events by taking care of ourselves.

> *Your body is the only place you have in which to live.*

Exercise is important. I used to schedule exercise just as I did family time and also gave it a number-one priority. What you eat, and how much, bears watching. After all, you do not put diesel fuel or suntan lotion into your high-performance gasoline car engine. It needs the correct fuel. Paying attention to what you put into your body is equally important.

It may seem funny to talk about family and health in a discussion of success, but it is not funny if you think about it. What is really more important in your life? Your good health uplifts the lives of those who care for you. If you end up a wealthy person with failing health and no family, are you a success? I guess a few people in this situation would consider themselves successful, but not in my life. Not in this book.

Including Precepts in Your Definition of Success

As I worked at defining success, I included precepts in my definition. These included moral and ethical things that defined who I wanted to be. They also included how I wanted to live my life, and physical issues such as where I wanted to live my life. They included family, how to spend my time, and how to keep my good health. These precepts might be seen as limiting the pursuit of my success goals, but my success goals *included* honoring these precepts.

KEY POINTS

- *Your definition of success should include precepts—those things including ethics, morals, and family—that you will do or not do.*
- *Precepts may also include trade-offs—things that require you to choose between mutually exclusive options.*
- *As you plan, remember that time is the scarcest asset, and is the ultimate objective in your quest for freedom.*
- *Good health is key.*
- *Include these nonbusiness items in your plan for success.*

WHAT TO DO

Remember, this book is about having a successful life as an entrepreneur, not just being a business success.
Plan accordingly.

PART II: FUNCTIONAL SKILLS

Kryptonite: Even Superman has limitations.

I asked Chuck Kersch why he joined Army Special Forces, which led him through a short, harrowing career in Southeast Asia.

"I was eighteen, and I knew nothing could happen to me," he replied.

Many of us feel that way when we are young—invincible, able to do almost anything, ready to go. Later we realize that there were actually some things we did not know. Our parents become wiser as we grow older. We become aware of shortcomings we have in certain areas.

Part II lays out the need to address several areas of business competence in preparation for your life as an entrepreneur.

CHAPTER 4

SELLING: MAKE SOMETHING HAPPEN

Recently I was riding into Denver from the airport and began talking with two young people sitting next to me. The young lady had graduated from a top Eastern college and was in her first month of working for the information systems department of a large hospital. I asked about her career plan and determined she did not have one. I asked what skills she thought might be useful moving forward, and she was not sure.

The young fellow next to her had graduated from a Western state university with a degree in information systems and was selling insurance. He was in Denver for a three-day seminar on how to sell insurance more effectively. I told him how impressed I was with his early career path. Not only did he have a background in a functional specialty for the twenty-first century—information systems—but he was now adding the functional skill of direct selling to his repertoire. He was off to a great start at age twenty-five.

Ben Kittay, the skinny sales manager from Los Angeles who wore no socks and ran our sales crew for a period of time, used to say that no youngster wants to be a salesperson when he or she grows up. A fireman, a doctor, a Marine perhaps, but not a salesperson. Further, our education system does not teach anyone how to sell. But as we go through our careers, we are continually faced with the need to sell. We sell our financial needs to the bank, our products and services to customers, our ideas to our peers and bosses. We are continually selling ourselves. Who is as likely to sell "us" as well as ourselves?

A Learned Skill

Selling is not intuitive; it is not a skill with which people are born. Further, selling is not a personality type. A friend told me she could never sell, that she did not have an outgoing personality. I told her some of the best salespeople I knew were very quiet, analytical people. Their skill was giving customers the information they needed in order to make a decision—and then closing the sale!

Our two sons each spent a portion of their summer after the eleventh grade selling door to door. It was hard, challenging work, but they learned the basics of selling. I went out and sold door to door after I had started my company and worked on my selling skills in this way.

Working on this skill does not require a major career commitment. It can be done part time, during evenings and weekends. But it can fit very nicely into a career. You can work for a company that will teach you to sell and give you the opportunity to do so.

What types of jobs will teach you to sell? Try selling vacuum cleaners or cable TV part time, door to door. Seek a full-time job selling real estate or insurance. A lot of young people these days get their start selling cell phone services. The key to any job that will teach you to sell is that it pays you mostly on commission. You don't get paid unless you make a sale. This concentrates the mind wonderfully.

A World of Opportunity

A person who can sell enters a world of opportunity, because almost everything we do involves making a sale. We not only sell products and services; we sell ourselves, our ideas, the way we live our lives. Work for a company, large or small. Work for yourself. Start your own company. Be a stay-at-home parent and sell part time. Go into politics. Serve your country in the military. All of these options work better when you can sell.

> *. . . almost everything we do involves making a sale.*

KEY POINTS

- *Selling is a learned skill.*
- *Almost everything involves selling.*

WHAT TO DO

Sell a product or a service, for a month or for your next job.

CHAPTER 5

MONEY: THE MOTHERBOARD OF CAPITALISM

An understanding of money—the role it plays in our society and how to communicate about money matters—is important. To get through life in this world it is useful to know about money.

Staying Ahead of Budget

Neither your business nor your family life will proceed as you hope if you do not stay cash positive. This involves more than balancing your checkbook.

As an officer in a large company some years ago, I had a meeting with a subordinate and his subordinate. They had asked for the meeting to discuss the problem of George, who was yet another level down in the organization. He was a great employee, but, as a family man with two children, he simply could not live on what we were paying him. I was very sympathetic, and we discussed various things we could do to get a significant wage increase for George. My subordinates should have closed their sale and left. Unfortunately for them, they continued to talk about the problem. As they spoke, it occurred to me that I, with two children, was living on less than

George's take-home pay. I was making more money, of course, but I was not *spending* it all on living expenses. I was saving the difference. If I could live on the amount of George's take-home pay, why was he unable to do so? End of meeting. It is always how much you spend and never how much you make that determines your financial solvency.

> *It is always how much you spend and never how much you make...*

Knowing About Finance

If you want to be an entrepreneur, or rise to a higher level in a company or organization, it is important to have financial knowledge. The performance of for-profit entities is measured with money. No organization, for-profit or otherwise, can operate over the longer term unless it stays in the black. As an entrepreneur, you will want to get to positive cash flow quickly, that is, to get past *breakeven* and then stay there. You will have to talk with lenders and investors along the way, at start-up and long after your company has become profitable. Theirs is the language of money.

What kind of financial knowledge do you need? It would be nice to be a CPA or a finance MBA, but it is not necessary. You do, however, need to know how to put together a set of financial statements—profit and loss, balance sheet, and funds flow. If you did not study this in school, a continuing education course at a community college or elsewhere will get you to this point.

You should also know how financial institutions operate. One of the best things I did in my career was to work for a bank, first as a management trainee and later as an officer. I learned how banks decide whom to lend to, how they process approvals internally, and what they do when a loan goes bad. This knowledge helped me immensely when I was on the other side, trying to "sell" them on financing my company (that is, trying to borrow money).

I believe a useful step on your career path is to work for a financial institution. This could be a bank, an investment bank, a mutual fund or other money manager, or some other financial intermediary. You might get the same education working in the financial area for a business that uses such institutions, but typically businesses have senior people manage these financial relations, so there are fewer opportunities for a new person to learn. There are many types of financial institutions, and many jobs within them. And before you take this step, get some basic accounting education. That one continuing education course will make a significant difference.

Finances as the Key to Understanding Issues

Imagine it is three hundred years ago, and you are walking on a forest trail. Two native groups inhabit the area, the Truthful Tribe and the Lying Tribe. The former are friendly and tell the truth; the latter generally lie and are cannibals. You see a native approaching you, and you nervously ask, "Are you from the Truthful Tribe or the Lying Tribe?" What reply will you receive? Will you learn anything you do not already know? Probably not, because both tribes are likely to describe themselves as from the Truthful Tribe.

As this story illustrates, many times you will receive information that does not answer your question, does not resolve the issue

> *If you do not understand a situation . . . , look to the money.*

at hand. If you do not understand a situation or are having trouble getting a grasp on why people are behaving as they are, look to the money. People's financial interests are a basic motivator of a lot of their behavior. Your knowledge of the role of money in our economic system will help you to understand what is really going on.

KEY POINTS

- *Stay ahead of budget by managing expenses.*
- *Learn about finance.*
- *To understand issues, look for the financial interest.*

WHAT TO DO

Take a basic accounting course. Consider a two-year stint working for a financial institution.

CHAPTER 6

"IF YOU ARE NOT A LEADER, DON'T LEAD"

I was skiing with a group of old guys when one of the fellows peeled off and went down a trail. No one followed him. We did not meet up again until lunchtime, when we found him waiting for us at the agreed-upon meeting location. "Why didn't you guys follow me?" he asked. For a moment there was silence. Then, from another of the old guys: "If you are not a leader, don't lead."

Leadership

When my son was sixteen and working to complete his Eagle Scout project, he had to mobilize other Scouts to come and work on the project with him on Saturdays. When my wife was president of a nonprofit board, she had to energize people on the board and others affiliated with the nonprofit to work on certain projects. When I was a U.S. naval officer, I wanted the best officers to stand watch in the Combat Information Center, my area of responsibility, so I worked to get my choices to concede their extra time (usually given in lieu of sleep) and take a watch.

Usually this section of business books is called something like "Managing People." In the social sciences the chapter is titled

"Interpersonal Skills." Many people call it "Administration." None of these titles work for me. I believe the skill needed in this area is leadership. I define *leadership* as "accomplishing things through others." Try looking for books, magazine articles, and videos on leadership. Amazon.com lists twice as many books when you search using the key word *administration* as it does when you search using *leadership*. Many books have the word *leadership* in their title but tend to be about every subject except accomplishing things through others.

Accomplishing Things Through Others

It is difficult enough to accomplish things through others when they draw a paycheck at your pleasure (or, if they work for you in an organization like the government, where they draw a paycheck whether it pleases you or not). But it is even more difficult when you have to accomplish things through people who have no obligation to help, as in volunteer organizations. I always worked to check references for leadership qualifications when I hired people, and more often than not I found validation in their successful nonprofit work. That is, they did not just hold a title for a year and put it on their résumé, they actually accomplished something while at the nonprofit. And related to the skill of selling, people who have been successful fund-raisers for nonprofits have obtained practical knowledge in direct selling, further enhancing the value of this experience.

Leadership from Within

I firmly believe in leadership from within. That is, one does not need the title of leader, CEO, president, and so on, in order to accomplish things through people. It is a fine skill to be able to move a group down an important path from a position within the middle of the group. It distresses me that so many educational institutions and recognition programs salute the head person, but never seem to take the time to ferret out who might have been the real mover and shaker. I think it was Ronald Reagan who said, "You can accomplish a lot if you do not have the need to take credit for it." I look for the kind of person who does not need to take credit.

Easing Organizational Stress

I believe any organization—and three or more people working together are an organization—brings stresses and strains with it as a natural thing. To the degree the group dynamic tends to ease rather than aggravate these stresses and strains, the organization is more healthy and effective. I would always ask, rather than tell, people to do things. Of course, they knew it was a "telling," but it seemed to make the days, weeks, and months at work go by more easily for all.

The Time Factor

Why am I so hot on leadership? You will not have time to do everything yourself—and you might not be able to do everything well anyway. If you intend to be an entrepreneur, you have to be critically interested in *accomplishing things* over the long term. There will be no one above you on the organizational chart whom you can ask for help when you are an entrepreneur. That is, either your subordinates address issues or you do. If you do not have the ability to address them, you have to rely on others. And if you cannot address your significant business issues, you will fail.

How will you be able to attract and keep employees who will be able to solve these issues for you? Through leadership. How will your employees be able to attract and keep similarly qualified subordinates? Same answer.

Administration, the organizing and directing of a series of interconnected issues to reach a desired result, is, of course, important. So are good interpersonal skills. You can develop these in a wide variety of venues. But the ability to organize and direct inanimate issues is not enough; nor is it sufficient if people like you because of your interpersonal skills. To accomplish things through others requires—indeed, is my definition of—leadership.

Leadership opportunities come along less frequently than other opportunities. If you hope to go out on your own, leadership skills are vital. So get some experience that allows you to practice leadership. As already noted, meaningful work within a nonprofit organization often provides a great opportunity to practice leadership skills.

KEY POINTS

- *Leadership is accomplishing things through others.*
- *It's possible to lead from within as well as from the top.*
- *Good leadership can ease organizational stress.*
- *If for no other reason, leadership is important because you will not have time to do everything yourself!*

WHAT TO DO

Develop your leadership skills early and often by placing yourself in positions where you can exercise these skills. Volunteer work is an especially fertile field for developing your leadership talents.

CHAPTER 7

MANAGING PEOPLE: MAKE SOMEONE HAPPY

When I was twenty-one years old I was commissioned as an ensign in the United States Navy, and I became a member of my ship's complement of officers and crew. I was immediately given management responsibility over twenty people, some of them much older than I. The rest were not much younger. I am not sure I knew just what management responsibility was, but I had it.

I soon learned a number of things. There were "doers" and "viewers." The "doers" got the work done. Parkinson's Law says, "Work expands to fill the time available." I found this to be particularly true with the "viewers." Just about everyone in both categories, however, wanted and intended to do a good job. My task in large measure was to help them to do so by working on the issues over which I could exercise some control, and trying to stay out of their way in the (numerous) areas where they knew more than I. Further, I tried to conduct myself in all my shipboard activities in a manner that would make them proud to work for me.

So I did some things right. For the most part, however, my first few months were a real learning experience. But it was having the opportunity to manage people at an early age, and gain some skill in doing so, that served me so well for the rest of my career.

Your First Management Opportunity

Earlier I mentioned that one of my nightmare scenarios involves the person who is a high-level professional or specialist and gets the big promotion at age forty or fifty. For the first time, he or she has to manage people. It is a case of "You bet your life." Would you not prefer to have had a little taste of this skill earlier in your career? If you are an entrepreneur, will you always be a one-, two-, or three-person operation? As you progress, will you have the leadership and people-management skills needed to keep your operation growing?

Such questions explain why I often counsel young people to get a job managing a shift in a fast-food restaurant. If not the career path you want for your life, it is nevertheless a wonderful way to build those people-management skills at low risk to your career. It can be done full time for a short period, or as a second job. And don't be concerned if you have to start by flipping burgers.

Learning to Manage

Managing higher-paid people and professionals has its own issues, but it is amazing how much of it is really the same stuff you work on with entry-level employees—and how often they are much more sane and reasonable than those highly paid "stars."

There are many skills you will develop while working your first management job. Just to list a few, consider:

- Hiring. What should you be most concerned about in making a hiring decision? How do you check applicant references, interview, and use other resources that are part of the hiring decision?

- Firing. When should an employee be terminated? How should you conduct the meeting where you fire him?
- In between. How do you motivate employees to work most efficiently and effectively? When should you praise, censure, teach, visit, or stay away from your employees?
- Wages and benefits. What is important to employees in the areas of wages and benefits? How do you conduct performance reviews? How often? What determines what you have to pay for a certain job?

The above lists just a few of the many skills you will need as a people manager. Your proficiency in these skills will improve as you exercise them. That is, when you seek a management opportunity early in your career you will not only be learning management skills, you will also be practicing them. Practice may not make perfect, but it will certainly develop your competence in the field of management.

KEY POINTS

- *Do not "bet your career" on untested management skills. Seek a management opportunity early in your career.*
- *Practice management skills on the job.*

WHAT TO DO

Get a job managing people. Now.

CHAPTER 8

YOUR SILENT PARTNER

Al Swift, a former member of Congress from Washington State, once told me, "Do not expect to ride around the jungle on the back of the political tiger without ending up in his stomach." That is, relying on government entities for your business success has its risks. So does ignoring them entirely.

Around 1990 Microsoft tried to be apolitical. It later ended up with a series of legal problems with the federal government and various state governments. Why did this happen? Well, you can say that the company broke the rules and was brought to task. I would suggest instead that it became too economically powerful without being a player in the political venue. Microsoft tried not to have anything to do with the tiger, but the tiger caught up with it anyway.

Shortly after my first company was sold in 1972, Seattle had a mayoral election. Because I had some free time, having just sold my first company and having no immediate work prospects, I asked a city councilman I had met, Lem Tuai, if I could work on his campaign for mayor. I would devote significant time in return for an inside look at how campaigns work. He responded by issuing a standing invitation to his policy committee meetings, and I went to work. It was a very useful experience. I had decided it was important to learn more about the political process. I had been taken aback by the degree to which politics affect businesses in this country, and I wanted to be better prepared the next time around.

Why are politics important to you and your business prospects? After all, you are not going into politics. You are just trying to be an entrepreneur, to get into a business and see it grow. That mindset is why you need this wake-up call.

Government Is Your Silent Partner

As an entrepreneur you will have a series of political partners in your venture. These are the various governmental entities that have, or think they have, a say over you. If you calculate carefully once you own your business, you will probably find that governments have a very sizable financial interest in your endeavors. It is not uncommon for government entities to receive a third or a half of your total revenues, if you include what they take from your suppliers. Governments generally take much more out of your business than you make after tax. But their interests do not stop there. They will cause you to incur expenses by requiring you to report to them and to obey extensive regulations. These laws and regulations will create contingent liabilities for you that will keep you awake at night and cost you money paying lawyers and accountants to ensure you are not violating these requirements.

These regulations and rules are seldom black and white, no matter how much well-meaning people think that they are or should be. Their enforcement is also a very gray area. At the detail level, you may have to work with a permit office, an inspector, or other petty regulator who suddenly becomes the eight-hundred-pound gorilla because of his or her ability to affect your business. It is not pretty, but the survival of your business might hinge on the way you handle problems with these individuals.

Some years ago a county official asked me why I was spending so much time at the county offices rather than out running my business. My reply was, "It is a sad commentary on the relationship between business and politics in our country. I would much rather be 'out running my business,' but what is going on here, right now, poses more danger to my business than anything going on in the marketplace; so my time is being devoted to these political issues, which are my highest priority."

Most unpleasant of all is the call from an elected official seeking contributions. You pick up the phone and you might hear something like this: "Jim, I need a contribution of X dollars from you for my reelection campaign." You might want to be a purist and announce that you do not make political contributions, but you have to remember that this person sits on the committee that is considering legislation that will seriously affect your business if passed. These are genuine ethical dilemmas, and you need some background to find your way through them. These things take place at all political levels, from your town to your congressional delegation.

Learning to Deal with Your Silent Partner

Every organization has to deal with politics. The above discussion gives you a sense of why I believe understanding the political process is a critical, key skill. You will still face the issues I note here, but you will be much better placed to craft strategies for dealing with them.

Gaining political knowledge is quite easy. Volunteer to work in a campaign, as I did. Surprisingly few people volunteer, and the "pols" will love to have the benefit of your time. You can also make this a career step by working in Washington, DC, in your state capital, or at your local municipality for a year or two. I guarantee you will see the world differently. I remember when our daughter worked as a page for a week in our state capital. At age fourteen she formed a very different opinion of our government than the one held by people who have not experienced the process up close and personal.

"Politicians and regulators find it much easier to nail people they do not know . . ."

You will find that you benefit from having an interest in the political process, almost without regard to what your business is. It will help you to understand your areas of risk and what you can do about them. My friend Gordon Macpherson said, "Politicians and regulators find it much easier to nail people they do not know, rather than to nail someone who is a friend." So stay in touch.

KEY POINTS

- *Every organization has a silent partner—government on the local, state, and national levels.*
- *It is valuable to learn how the political process works. Spend some time doing so.*

WHAT TO DO

Volunteer to work in a political campaign. Get involved on a local governmental committee. Or, spend a year or two early in your career working for government at some level.

PART III: THE DEAL

Are we there yet?

O pportunity knocks. Or does it? When do you reach that great crossover point, the time when your skills will be sufficient to become a successful entrepreneur? How will you know? Or, as small-business owner Tom Graham says, "If your ship doesn't come in, should you swim out to it?" When is it time to step out and become an entrepreneur?

CHAPTER 9

OPPORTUNITY KNOCKS

We had enjoyed five months of marriage and five months building a small cable TV business I started on the side while working my regular job. My wife and I signed a contract to buy a larger cable TV business, using a $30,000 note for the down payment. I felt it was time to become a full-time entrepreneur. We did not have $30,000, but we found a way. My ship was out there, and I was swimming toward it.

Business textbooks often describe this point with a graph on which the rising curve or line is your capability or collection of skills, and the falling line is your freedom to act—that is, how many children you have, how big your mortgage is, and so on. The idea is that when you get to or near the crossover point, you are most likely to succeed in your entrepreneurial venture. The graph looks something like this:

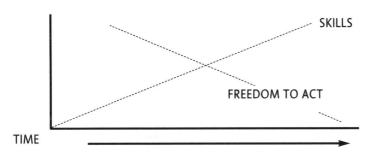

Of course, it is never quite so simple. The people who write business books know this. They just use the graph to make a point, and it is a point worth making.

Maximizing Your Probability of Success

In the previous chapters of this handbook I have suggested some things you can do to arrive at that crossover point with the most probability of success. These next few chapters are concerned with executing your transition to entrepreneurship by maximizing your probability of successfully closing a deal to buy or build your own business.

Maximize your freedom to act. Do this by keeping the fixed expenses in your family budget at a minimum. Your contemporaries may think you are not doing well, and that is fine. When we moved from our first home to the home we presently occupy, we did not put the first house up for sale until we had moved into the second. To our amazement, a couple of folks we thought were our friends in the old neighborhood became quite icy toward us. They had classified us as sort of working poor, definitely not doing as well as they, and when it became apparent that this was not so, they no longer cared to do things with us.

Thomas Stanley and William Danko in *The Millionaire Next Door* remind us that you cannot tell a book by its cover. You never know the financial situation of people from how they present themselves. Some people who appear to be on a tight budget may indeed be in that situation, but by choice, not necessity. You can be assured, however, that your young contemporaries who have expensive clothes, jewelry, two (three?) new high-priced cars, an expensive home, and mementos from their trips to Maui are not likely to be in attendance in ten years at the entrepreneur meetings you attend after you have become your own boss. Charles Kindleberger, in *Manias, Panics, and Crashes*, describes their likely future behavior: "There is nothing so disturbing to one's well-being and judgment as to see a friend get rich." Keep cool and pursue your plans without regard to what your friends and neighbors think.

It is never how much you earn, and always how much you spend, that determines your financial situation. You can better maximize your freedom to act, position yourself for entrepreneurial opportunity, and minimize your stress level by keeping your expenditures down, by flattening that declining line in the above graph that represents your freedom to act.

Manage your risk preference. In graduate school I read about an experiment that went like this: A person is taken into a room and given a number of rope "rings" and a board with a peg on it. He is told to place the pegboard where he pleases and to toss the rope rings onto the peg. Three patterns emerge. (1) The subject simply puts the peg on the floor at his feet and places all the rope rings on the peg. (2) The subject places the peg in one corner, goes to the other corner, and makes the long toss toward glory. (3) The subject puts the peg a little way out. If he gets a ring on it, he moves it further out and tries again at the longer range.

You have already assessed the three profiles. Number one is simply not very motivated to take risk. Number two is the speculator, taking excessive risk and anticipating a great reward if he by some stroke of fortune is able to get a ring on the peg. Number three is the high achiever, the pattern I feel fits most entrepreneurs. The point is this: *Set a realistic goal. When you achieve it, set a further goal. And so forth. Take reasonable risks in which you are likely to be successful.*

Dean Bill Sahlman of the Harvard Business School said in a lecture that entrepreneurs do not take large risks. For instance, you do not see them running back and forth across the interstate highway blindfolded. Rather, they take risks that have been carefully assessed, risks in which they are more likely to prevail.

Learn to deal with stress. Stress comes knocking with opportunity, and you need to be able to handle it. Have you seen those tables of stress points? They assign a point count to various life events such as loss of a parent, moving to a new home, changing jobs, having a child, and so on. You add up your particular point count and see if it goes above the level where the table says you may experience problems due to stress.

> *Stress comes knocking with opportunity . . .*

When I started my second company, I had just left my job earlier than my original plan called for, and had cash to cover six months of expenses in the bank. We were expecting our third child and were buying the home where we still live today. I was buying two very small companies that, operating together, would pay me an acceptable wage but less than I had been earning in my job—if I got the purchases closed. I had not yet financed these purchases. Let me see . . . What was my stress point count? Pretty high.

Of course, we all experience periods of stress in our lives. The important point, however, is the necessity for making good decisions under stress. No one makes good decisions 100 percent of the time, and I do not mean to suggest that you need to do so. You just need to maintain the same batting average you had when you were successfully climbing the skills ladder in your previous endeavors.

Managing stress is a necessary skill not just when you embark on your entrepreneurial ventures, but all through life. Stress is like blood in the water to competitors. They will use your stress against you if they sense it—and their senses are pretty acute! So always remember to manage your stress so it does not interfere with your decision making, and never project it to others in the business arena.

My favorite stress-management strategy was to do nothing until the next day. I would say, "Do nothing until I have slept on it," but I often did not sleep when I was wrestling with a big decision in a stressful situation. I would also analyze the issue in writing using the problem-solving approach discussed in Chapter 17. Talking with my wife, with close friends, and with attorneys and other experts who could provide me with factual input was very helpful. Simply stated, I worked harder to make good, analytically sound decisions when I was under stress.

Finding Your Opportunity

In my experience, opportunity seldom knocks. Rather, you have to go out and find it. But the idea, the concept often "knocks." If you continually consider and evaluate potential entrepreneurial opportunities, you will develop a list of potential avenues to pursue. It is then necessary to go out and pursue them.

KEY POINTS

- *Doing the deal is a big step toward the freedom you seek.*
- *Maximize your probability of success.*
- *Maximize your freedom to act.*
- *Manage your risk preference.*
- *Learn to deal with stress.*
- *Learn to make good decisions under stress.*
- *Look for opportunities.*

WHAT TO DO

Are you ready? Your ship is out there. Go get it!

CHAPTER 10

BUY OR BUILD?

Should you buy an existing business, or should you start your own venture from scratch? Both are viable strategies and require the same skills discussed earlier. I think both should be considered. You may locate a business that is consistent with your plan for success and can be purchased. Alternatively, you may have an idea for starting up a business that works for you. Consider both options.

Buying an Existing Business

Buying an existing business has its benefits. The business will have a track record that will help you to raise financing. It will have existing staff, products or services, markets and customers, and all the pieces that it developed over the years to continue in business.

On the negative side, some or many of these pieces may have problems. You might fantasize about finding a company to buy that is profitable, has no problems, and was owned by an individual who just passed away without heirs. These opportunities are quite rare. You are more likely to come upon businesses that are for sale because they have serious problems. If you understand these problems and have fixes for them that potential investors believe will work, then the opportunity might be a good one. If not, be careful.

Starting Up a Business

This option also has its trade-offs. On the positive side, you get to build the business the way you want it to be, rather than taking over someone else's concept (which, as noted above, might not have been a good concept in the first place). You may also be able to target an opportunity in the market that has not been satisfactorily addressed by other companies. Amazon.com is a good example of this. Jeff Bezos saw that books were not being sold in volume on the Internet. His analysis of this option suggested that selling books over the Internet offered many advantages over selling them from a "bricks and mortar" store. One advantage, for instance, is that Amazon sells more books from the group of publications with too little demand to be stocked by the large bookstores than it does from the group of better-selling books that are in stock at the bookstores. This phenomenon, called the long tail of online marketing, essentially developed with Amazon.

On the negative side, if you start your own business your entire initial investment will be risk capital. You will also have to finance much more "working capital," the monies you use for expenses and accounts receivable while you are working to get past the breakeven point. (Breakeven is discussed in Chapter 19.)

Opportunities for becoming an entrepreneur are endless, whether you buy an existing operation or start your own. These opportunities can involve pursuing an idea at home or after work, one that may not allow you to leave your "day job" for some time.

They can also involve the pursuit of a goal that does not produce profit. I know some people who started a private school. They never made much money, but they were as successful as any entrepreneur I have known. Twenty-five years later the school is an honored and respected part of their community.

Buying and building are two different things, but the entrepreneurial skill sets you will need, as laid out in Part I, apply to either option.

KEY POINTS

- *"Different ships, different long splices." There is more than one way to get into business.*
- *Buying an existing business or starting a business from scratch are both viable strategies and require the same skill sets.*
- *Advantages of buying an existing business include an established track record and assets, which can make it easier to find financing; disadvantages include the possibility of taking on someone else's problems.*
- *Advantages of starting from scratch include being able to target an unexploited opportunity and avoiding problems existing businesses might bring; disadvantages include a possible greater challenge in finding financial backing.*

WHAT TO DO

Consider both options, buying or building, as you look for a business to enter.

CHAPTER 11

HERE WE GO! THE DEAL

What is a "deal"? Since we are talking about business, we can use the *Webster's Dictionary* definition of a deal as "a bargain or arrangement for mutual advantage." Essentially it is a situation in which two or more parties come together to trade something each party has that the other party considers valuable. It can be as simple as your purchase at the pharmacy and that store's sale of the item to you. Goods for cash. In this chapter, however, we are considering the more complex deal in which you purchase or start a company and become an entrepreneur.

Some years ago, a friend of mine decided to take a year off and look for a business to buy. He asked me to be his financial person in this search, and every so often we would visit to review opportunities he had turned up. It seemed I always asked the same question: "What is unique about this opportunity?" That is, what is the distinctive asset you are buying with this business, that will be the generator of the success the business will have?

A distinctive asset might be a patent-protected product or process, a long-term contract to sell to one or more financially secure companies, a strong position in the market, a copyright film or book, or a building on the busiest street corner downtown. The definition of a business with a distinctive asset might exclude businesses such as a corner delicatessen, a real estate brokerage, and other easily duplicated companies. But these businesses might qualify if there is something in them that is distinctive.

Getting back to my story, there were a couple of questions I did not ask my friend. Perhaps I should have. I wondered why he felt so little tie to the industry in which he had spent fifteen years of his life. After all, that was the industry in which he had the most experience, the most to bring to a deal. I also wondered why he did not have an idea or two for starting up a new business. Starting a new business is always an alternative to buying someone's existing business.

Making a Checklist

Here is how I would suggest you go about looking for a business to buy or start. First make a checklist like the one below of items you are looking for in your deal. Your list may differ from this sample. Just be sure it includes all the factors that are important to you.

Checklist for a Deal

Yes	No	
＿＿	＿＿	Does it fit my plan for success?
＿＿	＿＿	Does it offer the prospect of making money?
＿＿	＿＿	Does it take advantage of my strong skills?
＿＿	＿＿	Does it align with my ethical concerns?
＿＿	＿＿	Does it align with my commitment to my family?
＿＿	＿＿	Does it align with my commitment to my community?
＿＿	＿＿	Does it align with my preferences regarding location?

Finding Deals

You may find this surprising, but I think finding deals is one of the easier parts of becoming an entrepreneur. People ask for guidelines and resources for locating deals. Where does one look? What categories of deals should one consider? Should one look at a start-up or at buying an existing operation? My experience has been that the deals have always been there, right in front of me. Many of them were not good deals, but if I kept analyzing each potential opportunity, every now and then one met my checklist of requirements.

Brokers and other intermediaries can be useful in larger deals, where a lot of money will change hands and they can charge a six-figure fee. Brokers providing these services range from the large investment banking houses on Wall Street, who work with multinational corporations, to "boutique" investment banks who employ a handful of people and concentrate on an industry or a geographical area. If you are looking for a business to employ only you and one or two others, however, investment banking type brokers might not be able to help much. Smaller deals simply do not generate enough money to pay for such a broker's time. What you will find in these smaller deals is usually just someone listing possible businesses for sale. This might be a small "business broker" in your town. Often it is a real estate broker who adds business listings as part of his business. Nevertheless, sometimes smaller opportunities can be turned up through these kinds of brokers, and it is worth the effort to contact them.

In looking for deals, you should routinely consider each potential business you encounter as you go through each day, and how well it fits with your checklist.

Do not approach the question of whether to buy an existing business or start up your own until you have identified the activity you wish to enter. That is, focus your search.

Controlling the Deal

When purchasing a company, controlling the deal will help you actually complete the deal. This is the way I approached my purchases. I would enter into a contract with the seller spelling out all the things we had to do before closing, when closing of the purchase would take place, and so on. I did not ask the seller to agree to a lot of contingencies, such as giving myself an "out" if I could not raise financing. I was a real player ready to make a real commitment, and this made sellers much more ready to do a deal with me. This approach helped me get the deal negotiated and completed. Of necessity it meant my deals were on the small side.

The issue is essentially whether to tie up the deal and control it, or allow it to remain in play while you go about putting all the pieces together. In the latter case you might lose the deal to someone else before you have tied up all your loose ends.

Controlling the deal also will help you control the future progress of the business you purchase. I owned 20 percent of my first company, and my investors owned the balance. When they decided they wanted to sell, I was obligated to execute that sale for them. I would like to have kept growing the company, but it was not my decision. I did not control the deal. Of course, we are all subject to our investors, our customers, our employees, and our other stakeholders, so no one is totally in control. But after my experience with my first company, I wanted to control my future as much as possible.

A friend recently raised a very large amount of money and purchased several existing companies. He is in the position I held in my first company. He has a lot of people working for him and a lot of assets in play. He owns a percentage of the whole operation and is essentially an employee of his investors. If things go well, he will do well. But he is not in control. His investors could decide to change their investment strategy, and he would have to start again with his entrepreneurial aspirations. There is nothing wrong with this strategy, and I believe he will be very successful. But I prefer to have control.

Making Money

In our economic system a business is supposed to make money. That is how it survives. If it does not prosper, all the other good things you hope to achieve from it will come to naught. Start by asking, "Does the deal make any money?" Seems like a silly question, but I cannot tell you the number of times I have looked at businesses that had no prospect of financial success. People still start them, or buy them, and go out of business.

Does the deal make any money?

My definition of financial success was to build value, as opposed to generating cash each year. Again, these are two different things, and each is valid. I was willing to give up more income in the short run in order to generate significant capital gains in the long run.

This is also a good tax strategy. Major sports franchises are examples of this kind of business. A friend who buys and sells horses, Milton Higgins, says, "Revenues usually only defray expenses. The profit comes in enhancing the value of the asset(s), and then cashing it/them in at the appropriate time."

I remember my wife once asking me, "If we are doing so well, why don't we have any money?" Even if your objective is to build value, there is still the need to generate some cash. The value strategy can also be difficult to execute if you feel spending pressure from your friends and neighbors, as discussed earlier.

Buying or starting a business that focuses on generating cash each year can also work well. These businesses usually sell for a small multiple of cash flow, say three to five times. Thus they are easier to get into but they create less value on the other end, when you wish to sell, because they will continue to be valued at that lower multiple of cash flow. These businesses are worth a smaller multiple of cash because they are easier to enter—that is, they are not *unique,* as discussed earlier. Because they are easier to enter, there are more of them—which means more competition—and the quality of management weighs more heavily in the success equation. That is, the more competition you must face, the better job you must do in order to best the competition. Examples of this kind of business include insurance agencies, telephone answering services, dental practices, and many other manufacturing and service industries.

Questions to Consider

• *Will your proposed venture be better financially than your present situation?* That is an important question to ask. In considering these issues, do not forget to "test" the financial prospects of your proposed venture against the alternative of simply continuing to work for others. You should have better prospects, both financially and in terms of other goals and precepts, from an entrepreneurial venture than from your present career before it makes sense to embark on the entrepreneurial venture.

A friend and former employee of mine started his own business a couple of years after I sold my first company. He was successful, selling his business for more than a million dollars. He then started a second and a third business, and was not successful. His money was gone. He continued to work at this business for several more years before he agreed to come back to work for my new company. He ended up making a lot more money in salary working for me, and he still was able to work on his unsuccessful business on the side. He would have been even better off had he invested his million dollars in a diversified portfolio right away and gone back to work for a wage.

• *What is unique about the deal?* I discussed this question earlier and come back to it again. I believe there should be something about a business opportunity that is difficult to replicate.

• *Is the price realistic relative to the prospects of the business?* That is, based on your financial projections, are you likely to make a lot more money buying and running this business than you would if you invested your money and worked for someone else?

KEY POINTS

- *Doing a deal gets you started as an entrepreneur.*
- *Your deal needs to be consistent with your plan for success.*
- *Finding deals is not difficult if you stay alert to possibilities that may present themselves in your day-to-day affairs.*
- *Controlling the deal allows you to get the deal negotiated and completed, and to better control the future progress of the venture.*
- *Do not forget to ask this simple question: How will the deal make money?*
- *Consider whether your proposed venture will be better for you financially than your present job.*
- *Ask yourself, what is unique about the deal?*
- *Consider whether the price is realistic relative to the prospects of the business.*

WHAT TO DO

Do the analysis. Consider the above issues when deciding whether to do the deal.

CHAPTER 12

THE DEAL: PART 2

I first thought of becoming an entrepreneur in a class in my MBA program. We had read a business "case" about a fellow who had bought a small company ten years earlier. He came to class in a three-piece suit with his Phi Beta Kappa key on his vest and answered our questions about the case. Even though this guy was probably a lot smarter than I, he had made many basic mistakes. You did not have to be a rocket scientist to see them. Ten years after getting into his venture, he was still living hand to mouth, and his prospects were not bright. He was happy, though, because he was an entrepreneur. I was determined to be a more successful entrepreneur. At the end of the game I wanted more than the title "entrepreneur." I wanted the freedom a successful entrepreneur should have, and with it a personally and financially successful life.

The Fun Factor

Why get involved in a deal if it will be a terrible drag? The inception of any venture brings with it an excitement that carries us along. You have to think down the road, however, and picture yourself in this deal a year or two hence. You will be spending a substantial portion of your waking hours working on your venture. Will they be fun and exciting waking hours, or will the business keep you awake in the middle of the night when you should be getting some sleep?

My wife made a comment that bears on this point. The University of Washington has a course on management of non-profit organizations for people who want a career in this field. Usually people are drawn to this area because they want to help others—a worthy objective. "They do not realize," Mary said, "that they will spend most of their time raising money." Many of these people enter the field expecting to manage an organization where others give them money, which they will then use to help people. When they get into the field, they find that they spend more and more of their time raising the money to pay for these good works. There is nothing wrong with any of this, unless you absolutely cannot bring yourself to ask others for money. If so, then "don't go there"—don't go into a career with nonprofits (or into politics).

BATNA

Do you know the bare minimum you can accept before you agree to a deal? Do you know your "BATNA"? If the deal never gets to a point where it will work for you, can you walk away? If you cannot, you are in big trouble.

A number of professors at schools in the Boston area got together some years ago and defined the term "BATNA," Best Alternative to a Negotiated Agreement. The concept behind this acronym is fairly simple. It says that there is some point beyond which you should not go in trying to reach an agreement. That is, you will be worse off after this point than if you do not reach agreement. The concept says you can define this point by defining your best alternative to reaching a negotiated agreement—your BATNA. That is, what is the best alternative that will happen if you do not come to an agreement?

Defining your BATNA helps you to define the point at which you should walk away from your potential deal.

Needs and Costs

Ask yourself: What need does the deal satisfy? Is this really a financial deal, one that will make money, or are you interested in it for other reasons? *Business deals must be financial deals.* But they can, and should, also respond to your other needs and goals. To do that, of course, they must be financial deals as well. Careers in the for-profit or nonprofit fields must also provide sufficient financial support to allow you to achieve your definition of success. If you are not sure, do the financial analysis—and listen to it!

Another question to ask is, what is the cost to you? We tend to measure costs in dollars, and, indeed, you need to consider the financial impact the deal will have on you. Are you mortgaging your house? Your family's opportunities? Your future?

Business deals must be financial deals.

These are serious questions. Happily, if you have developed skills and have a good performance record, you can recover from financial reverses. Indeed, a stint at being an entrepreneur might make

> ### The cost you cannot recover is your time.

you a more valuable commodity in the career marketplace. *The cost you cannot recover is your time.*

That last point is an important one: *The major cost is always your time.* Do not lightly mortgage a portion of your future, the time available in your life. When we are young, time seems a plentiful asset. From my viewpoint, on the other side of the middle of life, time is *the* nonreplaceable asset.

Liabilities

Take a close look at your proposed deal for liabilities, real or contingent. Real liabilities are easier to see. Will you owe money or be obligated to do things for third parties? Reviewing all the documents involved in your new venture should give you a handle on these real liabilities.

Contingent liabilities are more difficult to sort out. They obligate you *in the event* that something occurs. If that something can occur at the will of a third party, be sure you understand it and its consequences.

The most difficult contingent liability to analyze is the "unknown unknown," that thing you cannot know but which could nevertheless occur. By definition you do not know what this "unknown" will be, but you can test your risk exposure to unforeseen events. How might such an event affect your business? Your time? Your future? Will the business be able to withstand such unknown contingencies within a reasonable range of probability? Play out some scenarios, and see how the business reacts. For instance, you might assume that a third of your revenue will go away for some unknown reason. What will that do to your prospects? How will you recover? Scenario "playing" is a valuable tool in considering the potential future prospects of a business.

Exit Strategy

An exit strategy is a big consideration. You have to know how you will realize the value you hope to create in your entrepreneurial venture. Value is realized partly on an ongoing basis, and partly at the time you leave the business. The more unusual a business is, the higher valuation you will pay for it, as measured in multiples of cash flow. The higher the cash-flow multiple you pay to enter the business, the more of your value will be realized when you exit the business. If you enter a business with a low cash-flow multiple, one that is less unusual, you probably have done so to produce cash flow. In this case, you or your estate will still have to place a value on the business someday.

You begin realizing value at the time you enter a deal. If you pay too much, or embark on a venture with poor prospects, you have largely determined your future.

How is your exit likely to play out? You need to form at least two exit strategies before entering a business venture. Remember that an exit strategy will be executed, whether you intend it or not, when you leave the business or pass away. You can make a decision beforehand, or just let it happen and hope for the best. I believe you need to make a decision, and to do so at the time you enter a venture. In fact, you should have a couple of exit strategies, because the one you prefer may not be feasible when the time comes to exit.

Exit strategies could include going public; selling your business to a large company or to a private investor; insuring your life for the amount of taxes that will be due on your estate when you die, and then passing on the business to your heirs; and many others. Just think about what they will be before you get into your business venture.

Your Team

Doing a deal is a team sport. Sure, you can do a deal by yourself. You can also miss a lot of important considerations if you are alone.

You are probably not a seasoned player in every facet of the

> *Doing a deal is a team sport.*

venture you are entering, let alone in just getting the deal done. You need help from seasoned players in areas where you are not strong, be they finance, marketing, production, or something else. You also need an attorney and a tax specialist. I particularly like the idea of having an elder statesman on the team, someone who has been in business, has done deals, and will enrich the process. You will eventually need all these players as you pursue your venture. Why not get them on board before the beginning and realize the benefit of their input during the most important phase of your business—its inception?

How to compensate these people may worry you. Your attorney and tax person may be willing to work with you in the present, however, and wait for payment in the future. They are much more likely to want to participate if you have a plan for your personal success, a bag of skills you have developed, and a realistic plan for your new venture.

Other team members should be willing to be paid with a *carried interest* in your new venture, a small ownership interest that you give them in exchange for their participation on your team. Perhaps they will require no compensation at all. Remember your aunt who was very successful in business? Go ask her to help.

KEY POINTS

- *Don't forget that a deal should be fun.*
- *Consider whether you can walk away from a deal.*
- *Calculate your BATNA, the Best Alternative to a Negotiated Agreement.*
- *Ask yourself what need the deal satisfies.*
- *Remember that the major cost of a deal is always your time.*
- *Watch for liabilities.*
- *Your exit strategy needs to be part of your purchase decision.*
- *Doing deals is a team sport.*

WHAT TO DO

Invest your time in understanding all these issues before doing your deal.

CHAPTER 13

HOW DO WE PAY FOR THIS?

Two friends with whom I had gone to business school were putting together a venture fund some years ago and asked if they could use me as a reference. I said, "Yes, but what can I say to be helpful?" They said I should just answer any questions posed to me. Sure enough, I received a phone call a short time later. After going through all her questions, the caller asked if there was anything else I wished to say about these two people. "They are straightforward, honest, ethical people," I said. "They will take good care of your money, and they will look out for your interests before their own as regards your investment."

Your Reputation Will Precede You

Pretty powerful stuff, eh? It was true, of course. And it is what any investor hopes for when investing money in a venture. The investment really is not in the venture, but in the people running the venture and, most of all, in their leader. As an investor you hope to conduct a lot of acute analysis, make insightful evaluations, and choose good investment vehicles. At the end of all that, however, you are investing in the reputation of the people doing the deal. You trust they will honor you and take care of your money.

How do you build a strong reputation? It starts very early in life. People forgive errors in judgment when one is young, but they do not forget. They also remember displays of good ethics. When you are just starting out, all you have to refer to is your younger life, and your family friends will be your references. As you go along you build on that base and develop business references. But your good reputation is nothing less than who you are every day, in every venue. People do notice.

Investors need to invest somewhere.

Investors need to invest somewhere. They need you as much as you need them. They want to put their money with someone who will respect their investment.

Determining How Much Money You Need

When embarking on a business, or any other venture, you will always need more money than you think you will need. You or your financial expert will take your business plan and turn it into a financial projection. From this you will calculate your funding needs and your ability to repay. You should test the projection under various assumptions to determine what might happen if things become much more difficult than you had originally thought—the situation I discussed earlier called the "unknown unknown." This analysis can be presented as three projections: Best Guess, Optimistic, and Downside. Doing projections is a learned financial skill. If you do not know how to do this, you should hire or enlist the services of a CPA firm or a finance MBA.

Investors worth their salt will conclude that you need two or three times as much as you originally thought, if only because of the "unknown unknown." That is, they will be prepared to invest more than their original investment, should the need arise.

You might conclude that you can get this venture launched with little investment, and that you can fund it through a second mortgage, with your savings, or on credit cards. Be careful. What is that line from the movie *The Fly*? "Be afraid. Be very afraid."

Whose Money?

I always brought investors into my deals. At first I did so because I had no money myself. Later I continued the practice because of the discipline it imposed. Could I talk an investor into putting money into my deal, give him or her sufficient expectation of return on the investment, and keep enough for me to make it worth my time (time being my scarcest resource)? That was a pretty high hurdle, and only the really good investments cleared it.

I would suggest you not put your own money into your deal. If you do, you lose discipline. This caution is particularly important in your first deal. If no one else will put money into the deal, why should you? If your team, as described earlier, feels you should invest, however, then you should consider it further. By going "outside" you will have gotten at least enough input to

> *I would suggest you not put your own money into your deal.*

see the deal from viewpoints other than yours, and this will enhance the quality of your decision. Later, as your business grows and is successful, the risk of investing your own monies should have fallen sharply. Still, for major investments I would consider continuing the practice of seeking outside investors because of the discipline it brings.

Debt and Equity

Of the money you intend to raise, the more difficult portion to raise is always the equity, the investment in the ownership of a business. Debt, loaned money, is a first obligation of your business. All debt, interest and principal, is paid back before any money comes to the equity portion when a business is sold or otherwise wound up. It is possible that all of a company's assets will be paid out to satisfy the debt, with nothing left for the equity investor. Often debt will be backed by specific collateral, usually the hard assets of the business.

When you put your own money into a deal, you are investing equity, regardless of what you call it. That is, you may lend money to your business, but the other lenders will require that their loans be completely repaid before you can recover your loan. Thus your personal loan occupies the position of equity. Because equity is repaid last, this is the riskiest portion.

It is also useful to understand the difference between debt risk and equity risk—that is, the risk an equity investor takes and the risk a debt investor takes (per the debt contract). This understanding will help you contain your anger at your banker after he or she has refused to lend you money. Banks and other debt investors are not compensated for (or, in some instances, allowed to take) equity risks. Debt investors have to see a primary source of repayment (usually earnings) and a secondary source (the assets of the business, or outside collateral), and have to be able to sell their lending committees on the proposition that you are of good character and likely to try to repay the loan. They also have all those organizational rules, red tape, and politics with which to contend, and the likelihood that they will not be promoted if they do a bad deal.

Thus, as you can see, debt has its difficulties as well. In most cases you have to have an existing business, one that generates predictable cash earnings and relies on salable assets, in order to borrow money. Plus the good character thing. Plus the ability of your banker to sell your deal to the lending organization. If you go this route, help your banker to make the sale. Understand the possible problems. Equip your banker properly to sell your financing within the organization by spending time going over the issues he or she will face in selling your deal and supplying answers to the issues that might be raised.

KEY POINTS

- *You will need money to invest in your business.*
- *Investors need you as much as you need them.*
- *Plan on needing more money than you initially think you will need.*
- *Avoid investing your own money; seeking outside investors imposes discipline.*
- *Understand the difference between debt and equity.*

WHAT TO DO

Your reputation is everything. Never undermine it. Approach investors from a position of strength. They need you.

CHAPTER 14

LISTEN FOR THE FAT LADY

We had lunch and a beer in a small tavern near my office and worked over our deal. Then Bill and I shook hands to signify our agreement that he would sell his small cable TV company to my company for an agreed-upon price. I was pretty happy. I was also young.

A week later, I sent over the paperwork for him to review before signing. I received no reply. I called, and he said, "I've decided not to sell." Silly me. I thought we had a deal. As the saying goes, "It is not over until the fat lady sings."

"It is not over until the fat lady sings."

In retrospect, I had tried to get to closing too quickly. I never knew why Bill called off the deal. I would have been better off if I had spent more time up front "qualifying" him, understanding why he might want to sell, what he was trying to achieve, and what the impediments to closing might be. You have heard about "win-win" negotiating strategies in which the best deal is one where both parties "win" by getting the thing they hope to get from the negotiation. I did not have enough information to understand what his "win" was going to be.

If you are starting your own business, the need to close is motivated and affected by things such as raising money, buying from your supplier, and making your first sale. If you are seeking a new job on your career path, or raising money for your nonprofit, you still have to close. Perhaps you are buying a business, and you need to close that purchase. Perhaps you are selling your business, and you need to close your sale.

They do not teach you how to close in school.

They do not teach you how to close in school. However, good books and seminars on negotiation are well worth your time.

Getting to Closing

To me, getting to closing is pretty analytical, and it begins before you try to make the sale. Start by analyzing the other person:

- Why does he want to close with you? Does he have sufficient motivation to carry through? What is that motivation?
- Who are his constituents? What is the "victory" speech he will give to his constituents in announcing the deal? When we were analyzing a deal in my company we used to require someone on our negotiating team to make the other guy's victory speech for each of our potential offers.
- Does he have the financial capability to close?
- Does he have the authority to make the decision to close? Can his decision be reversed by someone else?

- Does he have a reputation for doing what he says, or is his reputation more worrisome? Some people think the agreement to do a deal—even if it's in writing—is simply an option for them to renegotiate a better price after the deal is off the market, and thus not available to other competitors.

Structuring Your Approach

Your ability to close any sale, large or small, also is a function of how you set things up in the beginning. Look at it from your point of view:

- What points can you control? Do they give you sufficient leverage so you come to the deal in a position of some parity, versus a "fire sale"?
- Define your Best Alternative to a Negotiated Agreement before you commence negotiations. Are you committed to your BATNA? At what point does the deal no longer make sense?
- Can you walk away from the deal? If the deal shapes up as one that is not good for you, can you simply walk away—legally, ethically, and emotionally?
- As the deal goes forward, is it structured so you are able to walk? If you cannot terminate the deal at any time, is there an outside termination date, a date at which you are free to withdraw without liability just because you choose to do so?

Money Talks

Most deals involve exchange of money. My chief financial officer used to say, "Money talks, BS walks." Your deal is not closed until you have the money in your account, free and clear. This is the definition of closing. Any monies that are to be delivered after closing are up in the air at best. These sums will require a second closing, carrying all the considerations of the first closing.

Controlling Your Emotions

Closing does not actually occur until you have the money in the bank, your first paycheck on your new job, or the donation from your nonprofit contributor in the checking account. This being the case, wait until closing occurs before getting excited. Do not change your routine, spend the money, or tell everyone about your new situation. To do so will put pressure on you to change your BATNA and reduce your control over the elements that will bring the deal to a close.

* * * * *

Any sale involves a closing, and the points mentioned earlier hold for each sale. Usually organizations will go through this type of analysis for a class or type of sale and come up with a standard way of approaching these sales. These analyses can be much more detailed than what I've outlined here. The point is, you make sales and get to closing by being analytical—not by being "outgoing," as a lot of people suppose. An outgoing personality is useful, but analysis is the key.

KEY POINTS

- *You are not "in business" until the deal has closed.*
- *Getting to closing involves analyzing your counterpart's motivation, constituencies, financial capability, decision-making authority, and reputation.*
- *Structure your approach to the deal by considering your ability to control the deal, your BATNA, and your ability to walk away.*
- *Remember, money talks.*
- *Control your emotions.*

WHAT TO DO

Stay calm. Remember nothing has occurred until the money is in the bank.

PART IV:
OPERATIONS: MAKE IT SO

Now that you own a business, you have to run it!

They say the two happiest days in a boat owner's life are the day he buys his boat and the day he sells it. The day you close a deal and get your new venture up and running is also an exciting day. So is the day you sell it. In between is the hard work. You may find yourself referring to this guide often during these years.

CHAPTER 15

THERE IS NO "I" IN TEAM

Running a business or an organization is essentially about delivering financial results within nonfinancial precepts. How you do it varies immensely, and the way you do it can have great value to various constituents. But the need to deliver financial results is always present. This almost always involves relying on the work of your employees.

Shortly after I embarked on my own venture, my sister asked me how she could describe to other people what I was doing. I said, "Tell them I am an entrepreneur." She replied, "That seems like a dirty word. Can't you give me something else to say?"

The Entrepreneur's Bargain

Most people have a fuzzy definition of *entrepreneur*. What does it mean to be an entrepreneur? To me, as noted earlier in this book, it means making a payroll. Sometimes I did not make out my own paycheck, but I never failed my employees. Making your payroll on time is the essence of running your own show versus working for someone else. It is also the entrepreneur's bargain.

Many people are risk averse. Many of them are great people and do great work; they just do not want the risk, the burden, the stress of worrying about their next paycheck. In return for removing that burden from their shoulders, they will work hard for you and allow you to charge your customers for the fruits of their labor. What you are able to charge for their labor, if you have a viable business, is more than you have to pay them for that labor. If that formula is not working, you do not have a viable business.

As an entrepreneur, then, you are an intermediary between someone's labor and the purchaser of the fruits of that labor. The purchasers do not pay for the labor each payday, because they are buying the completed product or service. As the intermediary, you pay your employees each payday and finance that expense until such time as you can sell the finished product or service.

When you become an entrepreneur you disintermediate your-self—that is, you remove any intermediary between the work you do and the compensation you receive for that work.

Enriching the Bargain

Employees. People work for money, but most work for a lot more reasons. If you have an employee who is only seeking the highest pay, he will soon be gone. Worse, he will work to move the culture of your company toward that "free agent" mentality. You want players who have a long-term commitment to your venture. How do you go about achieving this?

One way is to realize that most people want things in addition to a wage or a salary. They want their pay to reflect the market's valuation of the work they do, but they do not need to receive the highest pay for their work. They are smart enough to realize that the highest pay this year may not be around next year. They want things to enhance their career (especially if they have read this book) and seek them from your company. They want you to support their ability to have a life outside the company. Most of all, they want your trust and respect.

Supervisors. Most supervisors are poor leaders, poor people managers. This is not a permanent condition, but it arises because most supervisors have been promoted based on their ability to work effectively, not their ability to lead people. They need training, mentoring, and a constant review and upgrading of their capabilities. By helping your supervisors to become more effective leaders and managers, you will remove a lot of their frustration and make their work more rewarding, while at the same time improving the effectiveness of the portion of your company that they supervise.

Managers. Managers, for the most part, were once supervisors. As your business grows you will have managers and supervisors. You should not have every employee in your venture working directly for you once your staff gets larger than five or ten. These managers also need training, mentoring, and your continual work to upgrade their capabilities. You need to rely on them to help the people working for them to define and achieve their career paths, and to obtain the kind of life they want both inside and outside your company.

Employee Reviews, Benefits, and Bonuses

With as many as 130 employees, I always required that I approve any termination, any hire above an entry-level position, and any negative performance review. I often found that the manager or supervisor in question was not experienced enough to deal with the issues raised. These situations would usually benefit from my input, whether the end result changed or not.

We were not heavy on benefits in my company, but we worked hard to ensure that people's personal lives were not jeopardized by unforeseen events, such as medical problems. We had floating holidays, allowing us to be responsive to every creed and religion. We had no sick pay, but paid "personal leave" instead. This allowed all those people who never seemed to get sick to have the same benefit as their less fortunate peers—who tended to move on, incidentally, to companies with more generous sick-pay programs.

We had an array of performance bonuses that allowed those people who were particularly productive within the precepts we imposed to make more money. They were making more money for us, and we allowed them to participate in the success they helped to create.

Remembering Who Does the Work

I used to continually tell myself that if I did not have employee A or employee B, I might have to do that job myself. As my business grew, many of my employees were much more qualified than I was to complete their particular assignments. It thus became easier to define my CEO duty as working hard to ensure my employees enjoyed a good environment in which to complete their work each day. After all, if they did not do it, I might have to do it myself!

The Peter Principle says that people rise to their level of incompetence. One of the important tasks of a leader is to ensure this does not happen, to ensure people are challenged in their work but not asked to do things that might be beyond them. This is the opposite of the input most business books give about how to get ahead and how to help your employees get ahead.

A brief anecdote illustrates this point. In 1980 my company built an extensive microwave system to interconnect and bring TV stations into a group of cable TV systems we operated in a high-desert region of California. It was enough fun hauling cement trucks up a bad road with a D-8 Cat to a 9,000-foot mountain peak to pour the concrete tower bases and construct a building. I suppose it actually was a bit of fun to have to hike up there on snowshoes on a nice winter day to perform maintenance checks. It was definitely no fun to have to get up there on a stormy winter evening to fix a failure. And there were not many people who could do these checks correctly, who could fix failures. This required a new hire, a full-time person, and we brought on board a fellow who seemed perfect for the job that needed to be done.

As the months went by, however, I started to have the same conversation over and over again with my manager. He would say, "Fred [the microwave tech] is driving me nuts."

"Why?" I would ask.

The manager would respond, "He never tells me what he is doing, he doesn't get his paperwork in on time, and he never talks with the other supervisors. He spends most of his time visiting our microwave sites and playing with the gear."

"How is the microwave system working?" I would ask.

"Wow, has it been great! No failures, humming like a top, great quality. . ." my manager would reply. Then his voice would trail off as he remembered that Fred had been brought on board strictly to keep the microwave system operating at peak performance. Fred was a great microwave tech, and those people are hard to find. He had other shortcomings, but we had not hired him for those other qualities. It was the manager's job to enable him to succeed in those other areas. End of story.

In my business career I had at least two instances in which I significantly demoted an employee who then stayed with my company over the long term. Employees know when they are in over their head. If you approach the problem with trust and respect, it is not uncommon for them to agree to your concern and accept a different arrangement. (If they do not, nothing has been lost by trying.)

Help people to have success doing what they are able to do. Do not expect them to do the things they are not good at doing, and do not promote them to positions where their shortcomings will lead them to failure.

Building Your Team

The detail of building your team is laced through many sections of this book in summary form, and is an extensive subject in itself. These are the skills you will have learned and practiced in your earlier management jobs. Your team will be enriched by your attention to the culture of your organization, as you work not just to hire good people but also to add people who complement your existing culture.

Do not forget that the key member of your team is you. That is, there will be occasions which demand your participation if the business is to prosper from them. There is a story that pro basketball star Michael Jordan was once told by coach Phil Jackson: "Michael, there is no 'I' in team." Jordan is said to have replied: "Yes, but there is one in 'win.'"

> *. . . the key member of your team is you.*

KEY POINTS

- *The entrepreneur's bargain tells us that the entrepreneur is an intermediary between someone's labor and the purchaser of that labor.*
- *Enriching the bargain includes providing employees, managers, and supervisors with nonmonetary supports that help them do their job well.*
- *If you do not have motivated, happy employees to do the work of your business, you might have to do it all yourself!*

WHAT TO DO

Invest a lot of effort in building a good team, take care of your people, and let them do their work.

CHAPTER 16

COMPANIES, LIKE CIVILIZATIONS, HAVE CULTURES

My company was doing well and had attained some size. We sent some customer service people to one of our out-of-town locations—I will call it Xville—to facilitate a marketing program. A few weeks later, one of these people told her supervisor that she was being propositioned by the manager in Xville, who kept calling her up (during business hours, of course). This was reported to me, as required by our sexual harassment policy. We had that manager's boss visit him, tell him that his actions would not be tolerated, and that there would be no second chance if he did it again. He stopped calling the customer service lady. End of story. Or so it seemed.

Several months later, one of our customer service employees gave two weeks' notice, indicating she was moving out of town. She was a good employee and was treating us fairly. Still, I was curious. Visiting with other employees in the lunchroom, I learned that she was moving to a town near Xville. Further investigation indicated that she had a relationship with the manager, who had moved in with her.

I asked the manager's boss if he had any input. He replied that this manager was an especially good employee, but was having trouble with his wife. He said we should support this manager through his hard times. I thought differently. That afternoon we terminated the manager.

Why did I insist that this manager be summarily terminated? He clearly had violated the requirement we had placed on him after his previous incident. But it was much more than that. As concerned as I might have been for him and his troubles, I was more concerned for my organization's culture.

Every organization has a culture. You can shape it or build it to any model you choose. Or you can allow it to develop on its own, driven by the opinion leaders among your employees. But rest assured, you will have a culture either way. So the choice is yours—let someone else set the rules of your culture, or enforce your own cultural goals.

Previously I talked about employees valuing things in addition to their pay. I suggested they might value work that furthered their career, and a workplace that allowed them the life they were seeking outside of work. Most people have their own precepts, within which they try to live their life. These precepts are defined by ethics, location, religion, and other considerations.

People will try to work in an environment that satisfies most of their objectives and precepts. Thus it follows that you will attract to your company those employees who value the particular mix of objectives and precepts you work to protect and nurture. People who do not value these things will tend to go elsewhere.

If you are trying to assemble a winning basketball team, you might have to put up with an all-star who does not share your values.

Few other organizations, however, have to put up with this kind of nonsense. Indeed, if you look at professional basketball teams, you often find that it is the star *with values* who wins the championship, not the one with talent but no anchors in his life. As you go into your venture, you have the option to decide what kind of people you want as employees and, by extension, the kind of people with whom your employees will spend their time each working day.

Thinking About Your Ethics

My father-in-law used to say, "It is what you do when no one is watching that is important." We see Humphrey Bogart in *Casablanca* doing the right thing at the end of the movie. On the other hand, Spike Lee's movie *Do the Right Thing* highlights its ironic title by portraying a community where no one seems to do the right thing.

> *"It is what you do when no one is watching that is important."*

What is the "right thing"? That is a decision each of us makes. As I noted earlier, you can make this decision purposely or allow it to be made for you by the unfolding of events. Either way, a decision is made. Individuals choose their ethics. Sure, you can be brought up in an ethical home or in one that does not deal with the issue. You can innately know what is right or consistently fail to know. In any case, it is up to you.

I used to tell my employees that I would not second-guess their decisions as long as they did what they thought was right. Different people have different ideas as to what is right, but almost all interpretations are reasonable. That is, most people seem to do what is right. And it follows that you probably cannot set one ethic in your business and another in your personal life. Your ethic is you.

None of this is intended to tell you what your ethic should be. Rather, I am pointing out that we all have one, and most people eventually will figure out what yours is. Your ethic will become an important part of the culture of your organization, and you will attract employees with a similar ethic.

As you go forward in business you will continually find yourself facing ethical issues. If you have a good sense of who you are, by and large these will not be issues for you. If you do not, you might not even be aware you are facing such issues. Become aware, and calculate the cost of doing the wrong thing, especially the long-term cost.

It comes down to a simple question: Who do you want to be?

Peter Hart, who has been doing national polls for decades, said, "The world is a poll." That is, perception colors everything. How do you wish to be perceived, both in the present and throughout your life?

Operating your venture will be a long haul. It will be easier and more productive if the people who help you in that task have values and precepts that are the same as those held by you and your business culture.

KEY POINTS

- *Every organization has a culture.*
- *Ensure you are the person who sets the culture for your organization.*
- *You will attract employees who share the precepts embedded in your company culture.*

WHAT TO DO

Aggressively enforce your company culture.

Do not let others set it for you.

CHAPTER 17

PROBLEM SOLVING: "OH NO, YOU DID JUST WHAT I TOLD YOU TO DO!"

*M*r. Mack: *"If I had ten minutes to do a problem, I would spend eight minutes reading the problem."*

Ninth grade in the 1950s brought with it our first foray into algebra. Mr. Mack was my teacher. He had a florid complexion, and always wore a vest with his dark suit. Although he seemed large, he was probably not much taller than my ninth-grade height of five feet two inches.

I had a tacit agreement with my parents about grades: a *B* was OK. That is, while an *A* was great, it elicited little more response than a *B*. A *C*, however, brought down the storm, particularly if it was in a technical subject. (I was intended to be an engineer, as our country needed engineers.) Thus I was more than normally attentive to Mr. Mack as I started out in the world of algebra.

As our first big test was being passed out, Mr. Mack made the above statement. I not only got it immediately, but I have remembered it ever since. To get the correct answer, you must solve the correct problem, the problem at issue.

> *To get the correct answer, you must solve the correct problem . . .*

The importance of this concept continued to register with me as I moved through life. In college, rather than cram myself full of data, I worked on identifying problems central to the course and the issues they raised. In the navy, it was critical to spend the time available addressing the important problems.

Learning to solve the right problem is the most important lesson in this guide.

Identifying the Problem

Business is no different than school or the military in this respect. I cannot tell you how many times I have seen vast resources directed at creating a solution for which no material problem existed. A solution in search of a problem, I used to call it.

Many people also subscribe to a fallacy that I call "It has to happen, therefore it will," which requires you to simply put your head in the sand and hope for the best.

Much of what I did in operating my own company was to work hard on problem definition. What are we trying to accomplish? What roadblock has arisen, and how does it affect our progress? Just what exactly is at issue here?

And I always tried to remember Tom Graham's corollary: Inside every small problem is a large problem trying to get out.

So, it is really simple. Identify the problem before you start to solve it.

A Framework for Problem Solving

When I got muddled, I would generally go back to a basic framework that has worked for me through the years. It goes like this:

1. *Describe the present situation,* the status quo.
   - *Rely on "minimal clues."* What I call minimal clues are brief inputs that would never stand up in a court of law but that allow you to make a more acute judgment. If someone does or says something that hits you in the gut, go with that feeling. Do not overanalyze the present situation.
   - *Follow the money.* If a situation is unclear, it often becomes much better defined if you look at what is happening with the money.

2. From this description of the present situation, *identify the problem or problems.* If the problem is not clear, do one of the following:
   - Work further on the status quo, or
   - List a series of potential problems.

3. *Propose alternate solutions* for each problem or potential problem.
   - Estimate the cost of each problem or potential problem.
   - Cost-out each alternative solution.
   - Develop an implementation plan for each alternative solution, complete with cost and timetable.

4. *Review and refine* the above. You will find that some of the potential problems disappear, and some of the alternative solutions are the same.

5. *Prepare a plan to implement* the preferred solution(s).

6. *Implement.*

Note that this sequence of steps is a lot of work to go through for each problem. If you determine that the cost of the problem is small, you will probably decide not to worry too much about your solution. After all, your time is limited. If the cost of the problem is large, you will be pleased to spend your time defining the problem and its solution to improve your likelihood of success.

Implementation

When we were addressing a significant problem for the organization, we used to talk about "taking all of our aircraft carriers." This concept came from some reading I had done that said the Japanese had as many as eleven aircraft carriers available to take to their invasion of Midway during the Second World War. They brought only four, because they determined that four would be sufficient. As it turned out, more carriers would have made all the difference. The rest, as they say, is history.

U.S. planes from Admiral Raymond Spruance's task force of three aircraft carriers (the total number of carriers the United States had in the Pacific at that time) found the Japanese fleet while it was occupied bombing Midway Island. In an uncoordinated but effective attack, Spruance's planes sank three Japanese carriers. The Japanese got planes in the air and found the USS *Yorktown*, which they severely damaged. The *Yorktown* was subsequently sunk by a Japanese submarine as it tried to control the damage and get back to port. U.S. planes from the other two carriers responded by finding and sinking the last enemy carrier. With no air cover left for their operation, the Japanese withdrew, and the event was over. The war in the Pacific had turned.

I always wondered why the Japanese didn't take five or six carriers—or, say, all eleven. Surely the outcome of the battle would have been different had the Japanese done this. I decided that if there was a big problem to be addressed in our business, we would take all our carriers. If we could not take the whole "fleet," we would not undertake the initiative. Conservative, I know, but effective. If you maintain focus in this fashion, you significantly reduce your risk exposure and increase your probability of success. If it is worth doing, it is worth doing right. Take all your carriers.

KEY POINTS

- *First, identify the problem to be solved!*
- *If the problem involves considerable potential costs, follow a detailed scheme for problem solving.*
- *Implement your solution by "taking all your carriers."*

WHAT TO DO

Identify the problem. Create a viable, economic solution.
Implement your solution forcefully.

CHAPTER 18

COMPETITION: DID SOMEONE NOTICE ME?

As an adviser to a small company, I received a call from the company's very upset CEO. She told me about a major competitor who was calling all their customers and telling them lies about her product. "How can we stop them," she asked, "from spreading all these lies, which are very damaging to us?"

My response was not what she had anticipated. "That is their job," I said. "Even though you might not compete in their unethical manner, they are nevertheless engaging in the age-old practice of competing with you. Fortunately for us, they are doing two things that are very helpful. First, they are not competing very well, as customers will see through this deception and care less for them. Second, they are telling us that we have arrived, that we are on the map."

Competitive Reaction

Any modestly successful venture will receive a competitive reaction. You should understand this and not be upset when it occurs. It will tell you things are going well.

You will also need to counter this reaction. Because you know in advance that it will be coming, you can spend a little time problem solving before the fact, working through scenarios of what might happen and how you would respond to each of them.

A most important facet of any response is to continue to run your operation well, to continue executing your plan. Your first task in a competitive situation, then, is to do an even better job of running your own show.

Do not fight fires. That is what your competitor wants. Let a few of them burn while you continue to run your company well, develop your own competitive strategy and tactics, and implement them.

OODA Loops

United States Air Force fighter pilot Colonel John Boyd developed a scheme for dog fighting called OODA. This concept has been applied to tactical and strategic decision making, and it works very well:

- Observe
- Orient
- Decide
- Act

The key is to do it all before the other guy can implement his reaction. See what he is up to, orient yourself to the environment and how he is affecting it, make a decision, and implement it—all before he can. Your job is to stay inside the other guy's decision-making and implementation "circle," to stay ahead of him, to regain and maintain the initiative.

This is an excellent outline for operating in a competitive environment—which all business environments eventually become if they are having success. Plan and execute your business steps before your competitor can. Put him in a position of always reacting to you. Ignore his attempts to cause you problems, because you know you are about to launch another step in your program that will put you further ahead of him, further inside his decision-making and implementation OODA loop.

We used this strategy at my company, Summit Communications, Inc., while competing with Telecommunications, Inc. (TCI) in downtown Seattle. We *observed* by having people at various levels in our company talk with their friends, usually at similar levels, at TCI. By the way, this also is an example of how useful a consistent culture is, with everyone in the company on the same page, trying to push the business forward.

We would *orient* ourselves by routinely gathering and discussing this information—at least weekly. Based on this information we would make *decisions* as to what course of action we should be following the next week, month, and so on. As soon as a decision was made, we would take *action*. We were constantly ahead of TCI in where we were building, where we were selling, the services we were delivering, and so forth. They were constantly reacting to us. We ended up with 86 percent of this competitive market.

KEY POINTS

- *A competitive reaction is a normal part of doing business.*
- *To deal with competition, follow an OODA Loop: Observe, Orient, Decide, Act.*

WHAT TO DO

Expect a competitive reaction and prepare for it.

CHAPTER 19

ALWAYS COUNT YOUR DOLLARS

Breakeven

Webster's Dictionary defines *breakeven* as "the point at which cost and income are equal and there is neither profit nor loss." For our purposes here, I define it as the point you pass when your income exceeds your expenses. It is the magic kingdom of business. It is emancipation day, the day when you come into control of your own destiny, when you no longer need to rely on others to continue to feed your dragon. Given this, I have trouble understanding people who put off breakeven in pursuit of other objectives. It is like staying in college a couple more years, taking more courses you think will be helpful. Why not graduate and go back for a master's degree?

What kinds of objectives can sidetrack you from reaching breakeven? One such objective is expanding before the business model proves itself successful. This situation usually arises from the fear that someone else will capture your growth targets if you do not take your business into those areas right away. Another such objective is the thought that you have to build your team right away and pay large salaries before the business can afford them. Or it could be something as simple as wanting an upscale office with nice furniture.

None of these things will have value in the long run if your business is not successful. I believe that the shortest road to success is to achieve breakeven as soon as possible. As stated earlier, what matters is never how much money is coming in, always how much is going out. Tom Graham says, "The solvency of a business varies inversely with the quality of the front office décor." So let me belabor the point. Control your expenses. Stay focused. Get to breakeven as fast as you can.

Accounting Issues

Here are some important considerations in the area of accounting:

- Hire a CPA, and use him or her. Is this too obvious?
  It is amazing how many small businesses fail to do this.
  If you do not look at your numbers in financial statement form on a routine basis, you will not know where you are. Further, you will not be able to communicate where you are to others.

- Keep one set of books, and make them conservative.
  Track the flow of funds each month. It is too easy to get confused if you are including special considerations affecting tax accounting, regulatory accounting, investor requirements, and other things in your routine financials. Include the special considerations in the tax or regulatory filing that requires it, and only there.

- Have your chief financial officer report directly to you, be it an employee who is the CFO, controller, or bookkeeper, or your external CPA. This person is tracking your major family asset, your business. It is personal.

- Have a qualified person other than you and your financial person review your routine financials before presenting them to your investors, your bank, or your board. Do this not to audit for accuracy, but to ensure you are communicating the messages you wish to communicate. Do these financials really deliver the message that they are intended to deliver?

- Routinely budget revenues, expenses *and capital expenditures.* Capital expenditures, like expenses, are money out the door. However, because they find their way to your balance sheet and not to your statement of profit and loss, people often pay a lot less attention to capital expenditures than they do to expenses. Routinely and critically review budget to actual results. Delegate responsibility for delivering portions of your budget, and hold those persons responsible for results.

Capital

Follow these guidelines for matters involving capital:

- If your business will require additional capital investment from time to time, raise that capital when the market favors doing so—not when you *need* to do so.

- As you generate cash and other personal assets from your business, manage these assets separately from the business. Do not let your operations people "play" with your personal money.

- Estate planning is important. As you achieve success, check on estate issues and how they might affect your company assets and your personal assets.

Asset Preservation

Your financial person is responsible for your financial assets. Who is responsible for your nonfinancial assets? Have that person report to you directly, or through a channel other than the operating manager who is employing these assets in the business.

At my company we had very large nonfinancial assets in the form of cable TV systems that included over a thousand miles of physical wires and electronics running all over town. Our chief engineering officer had responsibility for the operation and preservation of these assets. He reported directly to me.

Things like insurance and contract compliance are also important in asset preservation. You will want to insure your nonfinancial assets, more or less like you insure your home, against loss from fire, weather, and other factors. Contract compliance relates to ensuring you abide by all the agreements into which you have entered. To the degree those contracts are valuable to the business, you want to be sure to preserve that value. If they can become a liability—that is, a cost to your business if you fail to abide by their terms—you particularly want to be sure to comply with the agreements you have made.

Financial Performance: The Measure of Success

The major way your business or organizational success will be measured is financially. Indeed, as noted previously, you have to be successful financially in order to deliver the other objectives you seek. Be attuned to these financial measures of success and what they are telling you.

KEY POINTS

- *Managing the financial side of your business is of key importance.*
- *Breakeven is the Holy Grail for every entrepreneur.*
- *Hire a CPA to handle accounting issues, and take a conservative, attentive approach to this aspect of your business.*
- *Raise capital during favorable markets.*
- *Keep personal and business assets separate.*
- *Do not neglect estate planning.*
- *Focus on preserving nonfinancial as well as financial assets.*
- *Financial performance is the measure of success.*

WHAT TO DO

Get to breakeven as quickly as possible. In your quest to make your business successful, do not neglect good financial management.

PART V:
"I AM GOING TO LIVE FOREVER"

Probably not.

D r. Ron Dobson's ten rules for a healthy life begin with "Remember that you are not going to get out of this life alive." This was brought home to me at age fifty-one when three good friends, including my college roommate, passed away. The doctor is right, so it makes good sense to plan ahead and think about when and why you are likely to want to exit from your business.

CHAPTER 20

WHEN SHOULD YOU EXIT?

Some years ago another fellow from my industry and I were driving up to go skiing. "Jim," he asked, "when will your company get to a position when you can sell out?" I replied that we could sell, but there were other reasons not to do so. The market value of our type of business was at a cyclical low. There was a lot of near-term growth that we had invested in over the previous couple of years but not yet realized. I had children leaving for school each morning, and I wanted to leave the house for the office at about the same time. I believe that kids do what you do, not what you say, and I wanted to model for them the type of work ethic they would need in order to successfully navigate life.

But you always have to ask yourself, when should you put into play one of the exit strategies you formulated when you entered the business? What follows is the analysis I went through to decide when I should exit my business. Like the whole theme of this book, this analysis was based on increasing the freedom I enjoyed. But first, what about your exit?

Your Exit

Part of your plan when you got into business was an exit strategy. You will have revised this plan from time to time over the years. To exit, you have to implement this plan.

Going public is the start of an exit strategy, but it is more likely a strategy to improve financing of your business. Operating a public company has an additional set of difficulties, which you should not take on lightly.

Family succession is another exit strategy. As noted earlier, however, do your children want to run the company? Are they capable? Will you be able to treat all children equitably if you pass the company on to one or two of them?

Most small business exits are accomplished through sale of the business. While each person will find different factors driving his or her exit, everyone must consider financial aspects. To put it simply, you should sell when the price you can get for your business creates more value than you can create by continuing to own the business. (Alternatively, you should buy when the opposite is the case.) In essence this says that you will have an opinion regarding the future prospects of your business and your industry that might differ from the opinions held by others. That is the essence of a deal. And remember, we are talking about selling your company, not the products or services your company sells. Selling your company requires you to consider the market for companies such as yours.

Factors other than financial enter in, however:

- Do you have other owners in your business? What are their desires? Has their situation changed?

- Is there a change in your personal situation?
- Is the business not in condition to sell? Perhaps you have started a new program that needs a year to come on line, or you took your eye off the ball and now find your financial statements are a mess.
- Would selling lead to greater opportunities for you without penalizing your investors?

Note that I do not list many things other than the financial aspects as considerations in selling your business. Be tough and be financially wise when considering your exit.

Continually review your exit plan and the options available to you. I used to do this formally every two to three years. I did it in my mind much more often. Do not get hung up on your desire to continue to operate this business. When the time comes to sell and do well financially, do so. As you get older, be more aggressive seeking exit opportunities. You are not going to live forever.

My Exit

Here are the thoughts I went through prior to selling my company. In the late 1990s our children were all out of the home, working or going to college. Looking at the large variations in value of cable TV systems in the 1990s, I sure did not want to pass away during a down market. Yes, my estate taxes would be less, but the negative of paying low taxes could be offset by the possibility of not realizing enough money from a sale with which to pay taxes or anything else! (From this perspective, it would be good to pay some taxes.) There was a real possibility that little money would be left for my wife's remaining years if I passed away suddenly. My company's debt was around five times annual cash flow. A year or two earlier we had told some of our investors that the company might not be worth more than that multiple—that is, a sale would bring about five times cash, enough to pay back the debt but leaving little for the owners.

Things were always changing in the cable TV business. When I went through this analysis in the late 1990s, cable system values had risen and were high, but one could anticipate that values would drop again before long. In the late 1990s these higher values were a function of anticipated cash flow from broadband Internet services. Would this cash flow materialize? If so, would it appear as quickly as the market was projecting? How long would these higher values last?

A sale during a period of higher values would accomplish a number of things for us personally. Primarily, it would give Mary and me freedom from business risks and freedom to do things in our retirement. One of my nightmares was the prospect that as we became older the business might be worth little and provide us with insufficient income. I had no retirement fund other than the value of the business. There was no large corporation (although some of their retirement plans are suspect these days) and no government entity to pay me a retirement benefit other than my Social Security. We had to take care of ourselves.

Some people think the government is going to take care of all of us. I do not think so. Remember the parable of the grasshopper and the ant? The grasshopper plays the summer away, while the ant works through the good weather getting ready for winter. Then winter comes, and the grasshopper is not prepared. I was unwilling to be the grasshopper as I approached retirement when I could be the ant. I have always been determined to take care of myself and my own. A sale would allow me to take care of my retirement needs myself.

Selling the company would also give me freedom from a bushel of risks. Of course I had been operating with many of these risks for a long time, but perhaps my tolerance for them was waning as I grew older. For example, the growth in health care expenses, content fees for cable TV programs, and utility pole rentals was forcing our expenses to grow out of control.

The whole area of government-mandated employee considerations was also a concern. Often laws and regulations ensured my employee would not be required to work and could return at a later date, but I was left to get the work done somehow. For example, under the Family and Medical Leave Act, employees could take up to twelve weeks off without pay, and the employer was required to continue to pay their medical insurance and return them to their same job upon their return. In a small company like mine, who would continue to do the work, to deliver our services, when our employees were away? We could not hire a permanent replacement. I might end up having to do the work personally. The ability to terminate a nonperforming employee was (and is) being rapidly eroded. More and more in our society, everyone has rights and no one has responsibilities. There is a great constituency for equality of condition, and a much smaller one for equality of opportunity.

And if I died still owning the company? Estate taxes would undoubtedly force it to be sold. (This problem will have been remedied if the presently scheduled abatement of estate taxes becomes permanent.) Such a sale in a down market, a "fire sale," would probably leave little for my wife and family, as I mentioned earlier. Their freedom might be greatly curtailed. Was I meeting my obligations to my family if I tried to hold on to my business for the rest of my life? I thought not.

Cable TV values were suddenly on the rise. I decided that to sell my company would greatly increase the freedom I would enjoy in my remaining years.

My doctor friend was right. At age sixty it was time to move out of my business and enter the next phase of my life. Happily, the market provided me with an opportunity to do so by selling my company at a reasonable value.

KEY POINTS

- *The most freedom you can achieve from being an entrepreneur can come in retirement.*
- *Sooner or later, life ends for all of us. It makes sense to consider why and when you will exit your business.*
- *Your exit will be a financial deal, tempered by a number of nonfinancial considerations.*

WHAT TO DO

Continually review your exit plan, formally and informally. Implement it when you can create more value by exiting than by continuing in your business.

CHAPTER 21

THE EXIT IS JUST ANOTHER DEAL

Selling your business is simply doing another deal, and the thoughts in the previous chapters on doing a deal apply. The main difference is that now you own the business, as opposed to trying to acquire one. Instead of being the buyer, you are the seller. This business may be the bulk of your net worth, what you are relying on to fund the financial objectives you have for the rest of your life. Be careful that you are actually receiving value for your asset. It is all too common for people to trade the asset they know and love for an asset with a much higher risk, over which they have little say—for instance, stock in someone else's company, as I did my first time around.

Protecting Your Assets

I believe you have not "sold" your company until you have converted it into a diversified portfolio of assets. In any other scenario, you may have simply traded your asset, your business, for another asset or a narrow group of assets that may carry a higher risk. Such a deal could well decrease rather than increase the freedom you enjoy. People make money by investing narrowly at higher risk. They keep that money by investing it widely at reduced risk.

Some people never sell their company. It is their intention to pass it down to others to continue to operate. This works well if the others are on the same page. These are usually your children, who may have different interests or different capabilities. You may have a plan for them, but they may not have the same plan.

Other people believe they are the "deity of deals," the unique individual who is able to duplicate his or her success ad infinitum. Very few people have this talent. One fellow I know had successfully sold businesses twice, starting a new operation each time. He worked hard and was smart. He thought his success was entirely due to his efforts, that he had the "con" on how to start and sell a business. He bought into and sold a third company. The fourth try, unfortunately, did not go as well. He ended up with most of his personal worth tied up in a company that was rapidly decreasing in value and that no one was interested in buying from him. He recently sold his home and downsized.

"How do you make a small fortune?" the story goes. "Start with a large one." My point? Be humble. The market is a severe taskmaster. Carefully assess your risk and the objectives you have for the rest of your life before you sell your business. Once you sell, invest your assets in a diversified portfolio. If you are going to go back into another business, invest sufficient assets in a diversified portfolio to take care of your future freedom and the basic needs of your retirement. Keep these assets out of reach of your new business.

Realizing Your Loss

Unfortunately, the subject of realizing your loss must be addressed. Economist and author Charles Kindleberger says in

Manias, Panics, and Crashes, "When riding a tiger, or holding a bear by the tail, it seems rational—but may not be—to hold on." That is, it may come to pass that your exit strategy is to recognize you have lost most or all of your assets and to simply take that loss.

Remembering that your most valuable asset is time will help with this decision. You may have lost your entrepreneurial endeavor, but recognizing that fact and realizing your loss will have the beneficial effect of returning to you your time.

What Next?

What are you to do with your assets when you grow old? Leave them to your children? Leave them to charity? Pay a lot of tax to Uncle Sam? We go right back to planning. Various options are OK, but you should make a conscious decision as to what will happen when you are not around.

The government has succeeded in making the area of estate taxes quite complex. Do not expect things to just "work out" after you are gone. Spend some time getting your estate organized and ready.

Leaving money to charity? Remember that by and large people who work in the nonprofit area have different values from the folks going to work each day in the business world. Take some steps to help ensure your assets will be applied as you would hope after you are gone.

KEY POINTS

- *Exiting is just another deal.*
- *Protect your freedom in the future by converting your company into a diversified portfolio of assets.*
- *Your exit may simply be realizing your loss.*
- *What next?*

WHAT TO DO

Your successful exit from your business gives you freedom to do all the things you had to forgo while you were working on having a successful family and business life. Enjoy your freedom!

AFTERWORD

Garrett Morris played the role of baseball player Chico Escuela on the *Saturday Night Live* TV show some years ago. The skits always featured Chico being interviewed by a reporter. Chico's answer to every question was always the same: "Beisbol been berry, berry good to Chico."

How do I feel after a career as an entrepreneur? I feel just like Chico. Entrepreneurship has been very, very good to me—full of accomplishments and challenges: starting my own company while I was working full time elsewhere; buying a larger company and bringing in investors; selling that company for stock and having to go back to work for someone else; starting another company in my basement while I worked full time; moving my business out of my home and into an office; hiring great people as we grew larger and seeing them mature and prosper with me in our business. It has been a great ride.

Entrepreneurship also has provided well for me and my wife in retirement. I now get to do all the things that were on my "list" earlier in my life but that I had to set aside while I worked toward my primary goals of family and financial freedom. We travel, do nonprofit work, and take on projects such as this book. And I have finally found the time to take up golf.

Entrepreneurship is not rocket science. It is like going through a door. You start by opening it. Open a career for yourself as an entrepreneur by defining and planning for your success, working to obtain functional skills, and then executing your entrepreneurial plan.

Jim Hirshfield founded Summit Communications, Inc., in 1973 and was the company's CEO for twenty-six years until its sale in 1999. Summit served 42,000 cable TV customers with video and digital interactive services, and several thousand more with Radio Common Carrier, Multi Point Distribution TV and Telephone Answering services in Washington, Oregon, Idaho, Montana, Wyoming, and Utah. Summit employed 130 people.

During his career Jim served as a director, executive committee member, and committee chair of the National Cable TV Association. He was inducted into the Cable TV Pioneers honorary association in 1988. He previously was vice president/controller of a large bank in Washington State and chief financial officer of two other Seattle companies.

Jim's volunteer activities have been concentrated in the education field. He holds a BA from Rice University and an MBA from Harvard Business School, and served in the United States Navy as a destroyer officer.

WWW.FORTUNEANDFREEDOMTHEBOOK.COM